Cat Tales

Ten Years of Feline Fun in *The Sun*

John Perry

Michael O'Mara Books Limited

First published in Great Britain in 2006 by
Michael O'Mara Books Limited
9 Lion Yard
Tremadoc Road
London SW4 7NQ

A CIP catalogue record for this book is available from the British Library

ISBN (10 digit): 1-84317-212-7
ISBN (13 digit): 978-1-84317-212-3

1 3 5 7 9 10 8 6 4 2

www.mombooks.com

Designed and typeset by E-Type

Printed and bound in Great Britain by Cox & Wyman, Reading, Berks

Dedicated to Norma, Tigger, Morris and Murdoch.

CONTENTS

INTRODUCTION

SUN readers have one thing in common with Britain's cats ... there are about eight million of each. Fans of Britain's number-one newspaper certainly have an insatiable appetite for the quirky stories about our feline friends that have filled the pages of *The Sun* over the past thirty years, with the newspaper having published thousands of nation-gripping cat tales since its launch in 1969. In putting together this collection we have fearlessly trawled the archives from the last ten years to come up with a fantastic collection of articles, each with the original headline as it appeared in the paper.

Cat Tales covers the entire spectrum of the feline form, introducing the reader to a variety of marvellous mogs and fantastic felines along the way. Read about Sadie the accident-prone puss who has used up five of her nine lives; marvel at miracle mouser Precious who survived 9/11 and was reunited with her owners after going missing for three whole weeks; admire the bravery of courageous kitty Scarlet who ran five times into a blazing building to rescue her trapped kittens; meet Purrdey, the vicious cat who has posties quaking with fear; and prepare to be shocked by the many fat cats and other extreme moggies living in Britain today.

CHAPTER 1

CAT-ASTROPHES: WHEN MOGGIES CAUSE CHAOS

CAT RINGS U.S. FOR A CHAT

A PHONE-mad moggie ran up his owner's bill by dialling America and purring down the long-distance line.

Curious cat Sidney contacted Ohio after getting his paws on the phone's redial and loudspeaker buttons.

Owner Margaret Graham, 54, also caught the feline making a series of late-night calls to her parents.

Margaret, of Fraserburgh, Aberdeenshire, said: 'I couldn't stop laughing – but he'll need nine lives if I get a huge bill.'

COP IN CAT FLAP AS PARROT GOBBLED

A HAPLESS cop who called at an empty house accidentally let in two cats who then ate the owner's parrot.

PC Kevin McGowan, 36, raced to a woman's home after her personal alarm went off by accident.

The owner was at work, but the back door was unlocked. And as the bobby stepped inside, two moggies who were sitting on the doorstep slipped past.

PC McGowan locked up, with the cats still inside, and left the keys with a neighbour, but when the unnamed woman returned to her home in Goole, in East Yorkshire, she found her parrot missing and rang the police.

PC McGowan said: 'She wasn't too thrilled with me. I just thought the cats were hers.'

Police bosses have since apologised.

CAT SAVAGED BY MOUSE

A SHOCKED cat needed a vet after being bitten by a MOUSE.

Burmese moggie Widgett thought it had the rodent cornered, but fled with blood dripping from a neck wound after the mouse fought back.

The victorious mouse then escaped into owner Marion Robinson's garden at Hexham, Northumberland.

Vet Christine Shields burst out laughing when she heard what had happened. Marion, 56, said: 'It wasn't the sympathetic approach I had expected.'

£5,000 BILL FOR CAT FLAP

DESPERATE Neil White went on a £5,000 wrecking spree when his two cats got trapped in an empty house.

Neil, 43, bashed in the door of the new £70,000 home,

ripped up floorboards and smashed tiles to rescue the moggies. He said: 'I panicked at the thought of them starving.'

Builders Weaver Homes let him off the repair bill in Barnsley, South Yorkshire.

YOU SCAREDY CAT

SPOOKED John and Jackie Bambrick called in a vicar to exorcise a 'ghost' from their house, only to find it was a cat stuck up the chimney.

The couple had already heard stories that their council semi was haunted by a poltergeist. And they woke bolt upright in terror when one night they heard a flesh-crawling wailing and scratching.

Housewife Jackie, 28, said: 'It was a horrible screaming that sounded like a trapped child. It was really creepy.'

The din kept the Bambricks and their three-year-old daughter Emma awake for three nights.

In desperation, they called in local vicar, the Reverend Paul Swann, who recited prayers and gave a blessing in the lounge.

Hours later the penny dropped when 34-year-old builder John spotted a clump of cat hairs near the fireplace.

He pulled out the gas fire and peered up the chimney – only to find a moggie staring straight back at him.

Red-faced John had to summon the RSPCA to rescue the puss, which was trapped 5 feet up the brickwork. They are now trying to find it a new home.

Jackie, of Old Hill, West Midlands, admitted: 'We feel a bit daft now, but there were rumours that the house was haunted. The noises were like something out of a horror film. Emma was really upset so we went to stay with my uncle. The vicar was very understanding and turned up in his robes to carry out the exorcism. Then John spotted the cat hairs. We took the gas fire to bits, looked up the chimney and there was a cat's face. It must have squeezed through a tiny space beside the fire and couldn't get out.'

John added: 'We think it belonged to a former tenant, but I don't know how it got in because I'd boarded up the cat-flap.'

Reverend Swann, 39, of Holy Trinity Church, said: 'God does work in mysterious ways.'

PET MOGGIE DIALLED 999

POLICE raced to Janet Mansfield's home after a 999 call in the early hours . . . from her cat.

Worried officers traced Janet's number when they could not get the emergency caller to speak to them.

But Persian moggie Tabatha had curled up for a sleep on the telephone table, knocked off the receiver and sat on the buttons.

Brewery administrator Janet, 57, of Burton-upon-Trent, Staffordshire, said: 'We woke to see torches shining through the bedroom window. Fortunately the police were very understanding.'

IT'S A POWER CAT

A CAT left 26 homes without electricity after refusing to come down from a telegraph pole for THREE DAYS.

The moggie sparked a rescue mission after it was spotted balancing on a tiny ledge 25 feet up the 12,000-volt pole in Montrose, Scotland.

Electricity was cut for two hours while the cat was brought down by a Scottish Hydro Electric linesman.

PURR OLD SADIE'S A REAL CAT-ASTROPHE

SADIE the cat is existing on borrowed time after using up five of her nine lives.

The eight-year-old pet was officially voted Britain's most accident-prone moggie after a string of scrapes.

Sadie's first near miss came when her TAIL was amputated after being trapped in a door. Then she fell into a waste bin and fractured a PAW.

Next she was nearly strangled when a plastic carrier

bag became wrapped round her NECK.

After that Sadie was hit on the HEAD by a bottle as she settled down for a snooze in the kitchen bin.

And she suffered MULTIPLE WOUNDS when a pair of scissors got stuck to her magnetic collar.

Owners Steve and Roz Price have spent more than £2,000 in vet's bills. Roz, 38, from Bradford, West Yorkshire, said: 'She's an accident waiting to happen. Since she was a kitten, she's been in the wrong place at the wrong time. After she had her tail amputated we decided to take out insurance with the vet. It's lucky we did because she's cost us a small fortune since then. The funniest accident was when she fell off the arm of the settee straight into the bin and fractured her paw. A specialist had to pin her leg, and she had to hobble round in a metal frame for eight weeks.'

Sadie won 365 tins of cat food after beating 4,000 other entrants in a magazine competition.

5p PUSS COST US FORTUNE

A COUPLE were given a cat for free, then paid out a fortune in vet's bills after it swallowed a 5p piece.

Roy and Kimri Pywell feared the worst when moggie Max became ill and several vets were unable to locate the problem.

An X-ray eventually revealed the playful puss had

eaten the tiny coin and he had to have an operation, setting the Pywells back £300.

Kimri, 24, said: 'I can't believe how much a free kitten and a 5p piece has cost us.'

Max swallowed the coin after Kimri's two-year-old daughter Elianna emptied her mum's purse across the living-room floor.

Kimri, of Callander, Perthshire, added: 'It was lodged behind his intestines and needed an operation to get it out.'

DRAT! I GOT £180 PHONE BILL OFF CAT

CLUMSY cat Persia trod on a phone and dialled up a £180 bill on a racing hotline.

The moggie activated a pre-set button which connected to a 60p-a-minute premium-rate line for FIVE HOURS.

Owner Nina Mortimer, 29, said: 'We got a bill for £268 and our usual bill is around £58 a month. It wasn't until we questioned it that the truth dawned on us. The operator said that ONE call was made to a premium line. We realised the number is "speed dial" number seven on our phone. Then I remembered coming down one morning and seeing the handset off the hook and hearing a voice saying, "Your next meeting is at . . ." before I replaced the receiver.'

Superstore worker Nina, from Hornchurch, Essex, added: 'Standing next to the phone was Persia. She loves to walk over the phone to her favourite spot on the window ledge.'

The call was made to an 0906 number that offers tips and live commentary on horse races.

Husband Barry, 32, a security guard, said: 'From now on it will be economy cat food for Persia. I don't even like a flutter. The number was already programmed in when we bought the phone. We have settled the bill but will take steps to make sure this doesn't happen again.'

A spokesman for the phone company said: 'We feel really sorry for them. It seems a remarkable chain of events.'

MY MOGGIE IS HISSTORY

WHISPER the cat is so bad at catching mice that his owner has replaced him with two 12-foot PYTHONS.

Max Burton borrowed the snakes off a pal after his cottage became infested with field mice.

Scaffolder Max, 52, of Mayfield, East Sussex, has sent Whisper to stay with his sister while the snakes get to work. He said: 'The cat even watched as mice stole his food.'

DOUBLE TROUBLE FOR PUSS

POOR moggie Ebony is dreading the next cat-astrophe suffered by his owner Sarah Walker because the hapless puss gets whatever illness or injury she has.

Their double mishaps started in 1997 when Sarah, 34,

broke her right leg. Days later Ebony was hit by a car and lost his back right leg. And all his teeth had to be extracted just after mum-of-one Sarah had her wisdom teeth removed.

Unlucky Ebony, 12, then lost his left eye – days before Sarah had an op on her left eye. They are also both on hormone replacement therapy and each suffers from asthma.

Factory worker Sarah, of Saxmundham, Suffolk, said: 'He's lost so many body parts he can't afford to lose any more. But I love him to bits – even though he has only three legs, one eye and no teeth.'

MIAOUCH!

WE'VE heard of a rat up a drainpipe, but not a CAT.

Inquisitive five-month-old kitten Harry got his head stuck while checking out an 8-centimetre wide pipe on a building site near his home.

The pet was rushed to a vet in Hexham, Northumberland, where the pipe was cut away under anaesthetic.

Harry was unhurt and is back with owners Robert and Sue Maltby.

Vet Tim Pearson said: 'I've never seen anything like it. Usually cats are so careful where they stick their heads. Their whiskers warn them when a space is too narrow. Cats are usually more sensible than this.'

CHAPTER 2

MEW-DINI: MOGGIES' GREAT ESCAPES

KITTY KITTY BANG BANG

MOTORIST Dennis Parker pulled over in a panic when his engine overheated, and found a cat lurking under the bonnet.

Stunned Dennis had done ten miles at 70mph with the secret passenger before his Mini Metro conked out. But the ginger tom, which broke the car's fan belt, escaped with just scorched fur and bruises.

Rescuers have nicknamed the moggie Smokey.

Dennis, of Edinburgh, discovered the cat after his temperature dials went haywire as he approached Musselburgh, Midlothian.

He said: 'I thought the creature was dead. It wasn't moving at all. Then I noticed it breathing. I couldn't believe it had survived, especially as I had been driving so fast.'

He called emergency services who rushed to the scene. They alerted SSPCA inspector Paul Anderson who took the cat to a vet.

Paul said: 'It's an amazing escape. I've heard of cats getting trapped in cars before, but not travelling that far.

I think what stopped the vehicle was the fan belt broke after the cat's tail got caught in it.

'Thankfully, the saying "curiosity killed the cat" was not true in this case.'

HUNT FOR LOST CAT IS RIGHT COOK-UP

RESCUERS spent more than three days trying to locate a cat trapped behind a kitchen wall, then discovered the miaows were noises from a faulty cooker clock.

Millie Emerson, 50, called the RSPCA when she first heard the wails.

They contacted vet Peter Dyson who used his stethoscope on the wall and announced that a kitten was stuck in the cavity between Millie's house and next door.

Firemen used thermal-imaging equipment and drilled 19 holes in the wall so that tiny cameras could be pushed through. They saw nothing.

Then Millie thought she heard the miaowing behind the cooker. But when a friend switched it off to move it, the miaows stopped – and it was then that they realised the truth.

Millie, of Kettering, Northamptonshire, said: 'We burst out laughing – though my kitchen's a shambles.'

CAT-ERWALL

BRICKIES working on a new house demolished a wall after realising a cat had been trapped behind it for four days at Mattersey Thorpe, Nottinghamshire.

CAT'S 45 DAYS UNDER FLOOR

A GIANT cat called Bruno survived after being nailed under floorboards for a staggering 45 DAYS.

The one-stone (6.35kg) bruiser's weight halved as he clung to life by eating spiders and insects.

He was eventually found suffering from starvation and dehydration after a builder heard his feeble mews while he worked in a flat near Bruno's home at Teignmouth, Devon.

The four-year-old puss – named after boxer Frank – is back with owner Aubrey Pitts after being treated at a vet's.

Aubrey, 48, said: 'I'm overjoyed. I can't believe he lasted that long.'

KITTY SPLAT

CAT-lover Sara Guy has renamed her pair of two-week-old kittens Wash and Go after they were rescued from behind her washing machine in St Ann's, Nottingham.

CAT'S 50MPH RIDE ON CAR ROOF

SIMBA the cat hopped on to a van roof for a nap and was taken on a 50mph terror ride.

He leapt on as driver James Marshall, 24, was fitting an alarm near the puss's Nottingham home.

Unaware he had acquired a passenger, James sped off for ten miles as Simba clung on to his ladder. When he finally stopped, the hissing moggie refused to budge.

So James drove the frightened feline to some animal-loving friends who coaxed him down.

After getting Simba back, owner April Allen said: 'He seems none the worse for it.'

CAT BRINGS HOUSE DOWN

DESPERATE Paul and Joanne Green took their home apart when their kitten Rocky vanished.

The couple heard muffled miaows so they RIPPED UP the bathroom floor and staircase, TORE OFF wall panels and REMOVED air vents.

Gardener Paul, 32, even SAWED a hole in the kitchen ceiling of his £50,000 semi in Tividale, West Midlands.

Finally, the frantic father of three rang 999. But even firemen armed with a thermal-imaging camera failed to locate the moggie.

Seven hours later, Paul heard a noise behind some bathroom panelling. He tugged it away to find the terrified kitten stuck in a waste pipe.

Paul said: 'We did hundreds of pounds worth of damage – but it was worth every penny to get Rocky back.'

PUSS-ENGER TRAPPED IN CAR

MIRACLE moggie Smarty went missing for two days after getting trapped in a neighbour's car engine.

She was only rescued when Stella McPhail heard her whimper as she zoomed along the road in her Saab.

The puss escaped with just singed whiskers after the ten-mile journey.

Stella, 53, of Aberdeen, explained: 'She was covered in oil, but OK.'

Smarty later went home to recover with owner Rebecca Stuart, nine.

CAT'S BIN TO HELL AND BACK

MIRACLE moggie Binnie cheated death five times in one day after getting trapped in a wheelie bin.

The desperate puss was searching for food when binmen came along and emptied her into their refuse wagon.

Then, after escaping from the jaws of the compacting machine – which squashes rubbish to a quarter of its size – the four-month-old kitten was dumped into a giant skip in Gairloch, Wester Ross.

Workers failed to spot her as she tried to claw her way to safety, and they drove the skip 120 miles to Inverness, where the rubbish was emptied on a landfill site.

But Binnie's ordeal was not over – she was then run over by a 40-tonne compactor and still escaped uninjured.

Operator Bob Fraser, 58, said: 'I could not believe that she was still alive. The compactor's wheels have massive spikes on them to crush down the refuse. Binnie must have slipped between two spikes.'

Binnie was later taken to a cat and dog home to recover from the traumatic experience.

POT BLACK CAT

PRITZ the potty puss was snookered when it climbed into a pub pool table and got stuck for 24 hours.

The pet even survived a bashing from the balls as locals played pool all evening.

It wasn't until the next day that landlady Sasha de Retana was reunited with her three-year-old black moggie when she spotted its paw sticking out of a pocket in the table.

Sasha, 29, said: 'She seemed to be waving at me to let her out. She had such a headache – she had been dodging balls all night. There were a lot of people playing and they must have wondered why the balls were a bit slow going down the pockets. My poor cat was bashed black and blue.'

Pritz vanished from The Blue Posts Inn in Burton, Staffordshire, as an engineer repaired the table.

Hours later, Sasha realised her cat was missing, but there was no sign of Pritz in the pub or in nearby streets.

Sasha spent a sleepless night fearing the worst. She said: 'The next morning, I heard a faint miaowing, but I couldn't work out where it was coming from.

'It was only when my barman suggested the table that I saw Pritz. I didn't know whether to laugh or cry – she looked so funny, but she was obviously upset.'

CAR TRAP CAT FLAP

DRIVER Robert Davies heard a strange whine as he reversed his car into his garage and found his cat wrapped around the driveshaft.

Ten-year-old pet Gemma was jammed in the engine and wailing for help.

Robert, 34, took a wheel off the M-reg Escort to try to reach her, but could not pull her free.

It took a fire crew, the AA, National Breakdown and a vet two hours to release the cat.

They dismantled part of the engine compartment, removed some of the suspension and took off the driveshaft.

Fire sub-officer Mal Fellows said: 'Gemma was wound around the driveshaft of the car and it was feared her leg was stuck and broken. When we arrived we gave the cat oxygen as she was very shocked and frightened.'

Finally the vet gave Gemma a sedative, which relaxed her body enough for rescuers to pull her free.

Lucky black cat Gemma's only injury was the loss of a four-inch patch of skin on her right side where her fur had been trapped. No permanent harm was done to the car.

Dad-of-three Robert, of Brierley Hill, West Midlands, said: 'We have had Gemma since she was a kitten and she's never done anything like this before. I will make sure I know where she is before I drive again.'

AA spokesman Simon Woodings added: 'The cat has certainly used up one of her nine lives. There is a lot of heat and machinery under the bonnet of the car which could have killed her. She had a very lucky escape.'

CAVITY CAT'S THREE-WEEK HELL

MIDGE the cat was rescued after being stuck in a cavity wall for THREE WEEKS.

Wendy Orr, 30, called in builders and firemen when the puss vanished into a gap behind the washing machine.

They dismantled walls, but all to no avail. Gradually Midge's cries faded and Wendy, of Marks Tey, Essex, feared the worst.

But RSPCA man Jim Farr kept looking and – using mirrors and a torch – found her jammed in a three-inch hole. He thinks she survived by licking condensation.

Jim, 42, said: 'She was tired, thirsty – but OK.'

WASH NEW, PUSSYCAT?

A MIRACLE kitten called Rascal cheated death after spending 30 MINUTES in a washing machine.

Horrified owner Elizabeth McCulloch spotted the soaked moggie in the washer just seconds before the high-speed rinse spin kicked in.

She dragged the mischievous seven-week-old pet from the washing machine and rushed it to the vet, where the animal made a miracle recovery.

Elizabeth, 34, of Gatehouse of Fleet, Kirkcudbrightshire, said: 'I thought he was a goner.

'He was sitting there soaked in the middle of all the laundry – everyone has now nicknamed him Hotpoint.'

Elizabeth found the stunned black-and-white kitten seconds from death when the final spin of her laundry was due to start last Wednesday.

She added: 'He went missing and I looked all over the place. I hunted inside and outside the flat before heading into the kitchen where I feared the worst. The washer was on and Rascal must have been in it from the start of the wash. I opened the door and managed to pull him out. He must have jumped in after I had put some clothes in the machine.'

Elizabeth's neighbour rushed the sodden moggie to a vet where he recovered overnight. Elizabeth said: 'It's a miracle he's alive. He was wheezing and water was coming out of his mouth.'

The plucky cat was eventually reunited with mum Grace and kitten sisters Reefer and Cinnamon.

Elizabeth added: 'He has fully recovered and has shown no ill effects, but I'm keeping him away from the washing machine from now on.'

PUSS IN GRATE ESCAPE

PLUCKY cat Bessie survived SEVEN WEEKS stuck in a chimney.

The tabby fell down the hole while exploring a neighbour's roof and landed on a ledge. Bessie was unable to climb up or down, and stayed alive by lapping up rainwater.

But she eventually got so weak without food she fell off the ledge and landed in Sarah Philip's fireplace in Shoreham, Kent.

Bessie is back with owner David Hutchins. He said: 'It's a miracle she survived.'

INTERCITY KITTY

A CAT that got stuck in a railway track miraculously survived by dodging 90 trains in two days.

The black-and-white tomcat got his front paws jammed as he wandered across the line – one of the busiest in the country.

For the next 48 hours the moggie had to crouch down as trains thundered over the top of him every 15 minutes.

He was finally rescued after a man walking his dog spotted him shivering under a sleeper.

Railtrack shut the line near Hebden Bridge, West Yorkshire, so the RSPCA could rescue the stricken cat.

The moggie – named Ivor by vets after children's TV character Ivor the Engine – underwent surgery because the wheels of one train had severed a rear leg.

But five days after he was rescued, two-year-old Ivor was up and about again.

RSPCA inspector Amanda Ashton, who rescued Ivor, said: 'He's amazing. He must have been there for at least two days. I thought he was dead – but then he opened his eyes.'

RSPCA staff have been unable to find Ivor's owner.

CAT RESCUED FROM 9/11 RUBBLE

A CAT has been found alive amid the rubble of the World Trade Centre after being missing for almost three weeks.

Persian Precious has eye injuries, burnt paws and has lost two pounds.

But her owner DJ Kerr said: 'It's a miracle. I can't believe she's alive. I gave her turkey, her favourite food, and she was starving. She's purring now.'

Mrs Kerr and husband Steve were with friends when the suicide hijackers caused devastation in New York on 11 September.

The rubble came crashing down on the block where they lived across the street from the Trade Centre. Then, 18 days later, rescuers were told a cat was heard crying near the seven-storey building – and they found Precious.

The pet was treated by the Society for the Prevention of Cruelty to Animals, who have also been helping exhausted rescue dogs.

Spokesman Roy Gross said: 'This is the first good story

we've heard. She has sores on her mouth from drinking out of puddles. She's dirty and dehydrated and her eyes are injured. Her paws are burnt on the bottom because parts of the building were so hot. But she's alive.'

PURR-SIL IN WASH

SUGAR the kitten is a picture of health after surviving a 90-minute spin in a washing machine.

The eight-week-old moggie crawled inside unseen, as owner Janice Thornton, 40, of Colchester, Essex, loaded in clothes.

Sugar was found unconscious three hours later. Vet Helene Johnsen treated her and said: 'Her recovery is utterly astonishing.'

CAT'S AN AMAZING ESCAPE

A SIX-week-old kitten astounded vets by surviving a 16-day transatlantic journey trapped in a shipping container.

The moggie travelled 2,500 miles from Canada to England without food or water. Vets believe the cat – named Villy after Canadian racing driver Jacques Villeneuve – avoided death by licking drops of moisture on the walls.

After sneaking into the 40-foot container filled with carpet, Villy was shipped to Liverpool. Desperately weak, she was then driven 100 miles to JHS Carpets in Tamworth, Staffordshire, where a forklift-truck driver spotted her.

Now on the mend, she will spend six months in quarantine before a new owner can be found.

Lorraine Grove, who is caring for Villy at an animal centre, chose the name because her hubby is a Formula 1 fan. She said: 'Villy must have used eight of her lives.'

SAVED IN THE NECK OF TIME

A CAT survived SEVEN WEEKS without food or water – trapped by the neck in the rafters of a garage.

Vets believe three-year-old moggie Kyle cheated death by licking the condensation formed on cold nights on the underside of the tiles.

His ordeal only came to an end when the garage owner heard the distressed puss in the roof space and alerted the SSPCA. He was rescued and reunited with owner Judith Auld who had given him up for dead.

SSPCA spokeswoman Doreen Graham said: 'He was desperately weak and thin, and unable to move because of the way he was caught.'

Kyle went missing while staying at Judith's mum's in Dollar, Clackmannanshire, when Judith went on holiday.

Human resources manager Judith, 39, of Edinburgh, said: 'He's been there lots of times before, but this time something spooked him and he didn't come back. When I went to the vet's to see if it was Kyle, I hardly recognised him, although he recognised me at once.'

The mum of two added: 'He was a shadow of his former self. He will need plenty of TLC – but we can certainly give him that.'

Vet Kenny Laing, who treated Kyle, said: 'I've seen nothing like it in 14 years of practice.'

GET MIAOWT!

CRUNCHIE the pub cat went missing for a week – stuck inside the pool table.

The curious ginger moggie crept in unseen when landlord Paul Hornsby took out the coin tray to empty it.

He was so frantic with worry when he could not find his pet that his wife Erica stuck 'missing' posters everywhere to try to track the cat down.

And after hearing faint miaowing, Paul even ripped up the floorboards in four rooms at his seaside pub in Cornwall.

A week later, when he had almost given up hope, the landlord emptied the table again and found Crunchie tired and hungry.

Paul, 60, who runs the Pirate Inn in the village of

Alverton near Penzance, said: 'I just couldn't believe it. She didn't jump out straight away. But when I turned back to put the coin drawer in, she was sitting there by the table. I had to do a double-take. I then realised where she must have been. She looked forlorn and was very thirsty, but she is quite fit. After a few hours she was back to her old self. She must have been petrified when all the balls were going down.'

Crunchie is no longer so curious. Paul said: 'She won't go near the table.'

LET MIAOWED

A CAT dozing in a washing machine was spun for 60 minutes at 40°C – and LIVED.

Tabby Toreilles was curled up in some laundry in the neighbour's machine when it was switched on.

Shocked Caroline Law spotted him just as the wash cycle ended. She rushed him to a vet in Horfield, Bristol. Incredibly, the cat came clean through his ordeal apart from a few cuts.

Care assistant Caroline, 22, said: 'When I saw him he was wrapped in a sheet and pressed up against the glass. I didn't think he'd make it.'

Relieved owner Debbie Sainsbury, 44 – mum to Fleur, ten, and Kit, eight – said: 'It's amazing.' Vet Sheelagh Houlden said: 'He's lucky to be alive.'

LOST CAT FLOORED

MIRACLE moggie Dandy has been found trapped under floorboards TWO MONTHS after being lost.

Clive Newman, 69, was shocked when his four-year-old pedigree cat turned up in a house a quarter of a mile away.

Floorboards had to be removed to rescue the pet. The RSPCA's Gwyneth David said: 'It's a miracle he survived.'

Clive, of Cheltenham, Gloucestershire, was able to be contacted as Dandy is micro-chipped.

PCs ESCORT CAR-TRAP MOGGIE

COPS came to the rescue of a kitten trapped in a car engine by escorting the vehicle to their nick with blue lights flashing.

The moggie – dubbed Lucky – got into Dave Savage's Land Rover as he waited in traffic.

He saw her dash underneath and realised she had got stuck in the engine compartment.

Dave, 53, who was shopping with wife Joy, tried in vain to coax the animal out and flagged down a police car.

The officers could not free Lucky, so they escorted the Land Rover at 5mph to the nick, which was a quarter of a mile away in Barnstaple, Devon.

Joy, 52, jogged behind her husband's motor in case Lucky fell out. The cat emerged unhurt.

Joy, of Barnstaple, said: 'She was howling her heart out. I could almost see her nine lives flitting away.'

Cops are trying to trace Lucky's owners.

'999' DOG SAVES CAT

A KITTEN hiding up a chimney for five days was finally coaxed down by a fireman who barked at her like a DOG.

Curious Smirnoff got stuck on a ledge hours after arriving at its new home.

The RSPCA were called but failed to entice her down. After five days inspectors feared the five-month-old would die and called the fire brigade in Penzance, Cornwall.

Fireman Charlie Jamieson went on to the roof, barked down the chimney, and Smirnoff suddenly reappeared.

Owner Jo Barker, 22, said: 'He sounded more like a monkey – but it worked.'

THE WEIGHT ESCAPE

A FAT cat lost 11lb when she got trapped under floorboards for five weeks.

Moggie Parsley tipped the scales at a whopping 12lb when she squeezed into an air vent which was then covered up.

But when builders heard her miaows and rescued her weeks later, she weighed just 1lb.

Owner Hazel Conder, 35, of Dufftown, Morayshire, told how her searches for Parsley came to nothing after the cat went missing. She said: 'Weeks later, a builder working on our neighbour's house found Parsley. She was very weak.'

Teacher Hazel added: 'She is now leading a life of luxury and is getting the best cat food and cream.'

A spokeswoman for the SSPCA said: 'Parsley probably survived by licking moisture off the walls.'

CHAPTER 3

CAT BURGLARS: WHEN PUSSIES TURN TO CRIME

YOU'VE BEEN MOGGED

A CAT burglar who has been pulling off nightly raids on homes in a quiet village has been identified . . . as a cat.

Blackie the moggie's haul has included blouses, shirts, slippers, shoes, curtains, scarves, gloves and kitchen utensils.

His owner, Mayor Audrey Williamson, got so fed up finding his swag in her backyard that she finally blew the whistle on him in the parish magazine.

Retired postmistress Audrey wrote: 'I wish to disclaim any responsibility for a well-known criminal in the shape of a cat burglar. In the past, I have been able to return most of the articles he has brought to the house, such as a pan scrubber, table napkins, blouses, shirts, and recently shoes and sandals. This deviant cat has now turned his attention to gardening gloves. To date I have two and a half pairs of the cloth type, three and a half pairs of the heavy-duty red type, some splashed with white paint, size 8. If anyone has lost these articles please let me know before the police pay me a visit.'

Audrey, who took in the cheeky stray just over a year

ago in Much Wenlock, Shropshire, said: 'It's very embarrassing. The only person he doesn't seem to steal from is me.'

Neighbour Angela Cook, 38, said: 'We thought there was a prowler. Now we know it's Blackie our minds are at rest. He's a cute little cat and no one could get angry with him.'

PC Gordon Walker, of Much Wenlock police, said: 'I can confirm Blackie will not be questioned or arrested.'

CAT BURGLAR ATE MY RING

FRANTIC Jo Taylor searched high and low for her engagement ring, then realised it had been eaten by her cat.

The £400 diamond sparkler vanished from a bedside table after Jo, 27, took it off for the night.

The nursery nurse suspected moggie Hester had gulped it down and took her to a vet, but he pooh-poohed the idea.

Jo spent another four days searching her mum-in-law's home – where she and husband Sean, 33, had been staying – and even called the police.

But when Hester got sick an increasingly worried Jo took her back to vet Tim Wingfield.

He spotted the ring on an X-ray and operated on Hester to remove it.

Give a cat a phone: clumsy feline Persia ran up a whopping £180 phone bill after accidentally dialling a 60p-a-minute premium-rate racing hotline for five hours.

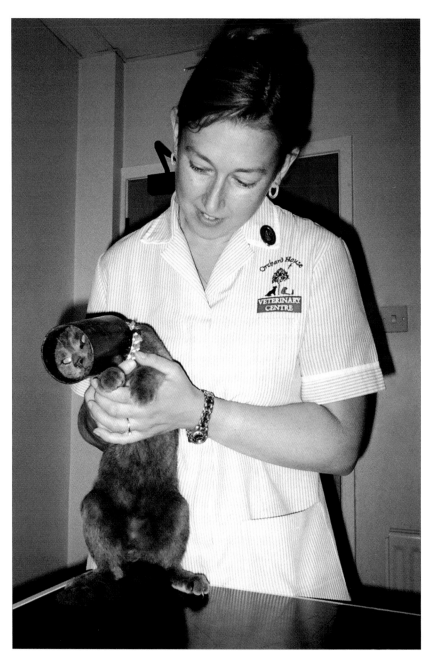

What a catastrophe: Harry the five-month-old kitten, who got his head trapped in a drainpipe near his home, is looked after by a nurse at Orchard House Veterinary Centre, Northumberland.

John Major's runaway moggie Humphrey was found safe and sound just 24 hours after he was declared 'Missing, presumed dead'.

Above: No Tom and Jerry: Mickey the Mouse and friendly feline Emma share a tender miaow-ment.

Right: Giant mouser Thomas refuses to go on a diet, instead scoffing his way through four meals a day. At 28lb (2 stone), the ten-year-old feline is one of the fattest cats in Britain.

Fat Cat: mighty moggie Zac weighs in at a puss-itively enormous 28lb. Owner Neville King tried unsuccessfully to put Zac on a diet and now feeds the greedy feline whenever he's hungry.

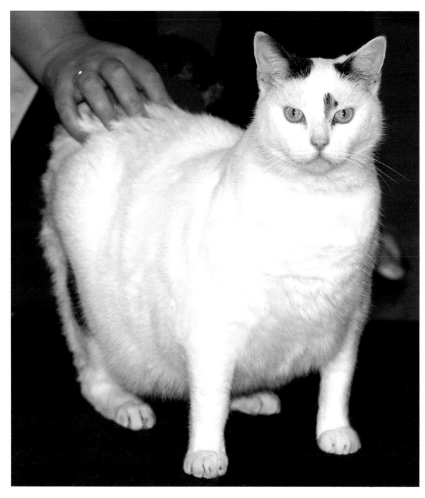

Munching moggie Fidget is a giant tab of lard! Chomping his way through bags of food at the pet shop where he was dumped as a kitten, the podgy puss now weighs in at a staggering 18lb.

Bulging Barney, a Tom cat from Porton, Staffordshire, weighs in at a whopping 24lb.

Face Oddity: Siamese cat David Miaowie shows off his distinctive facial features. The odd-looking puss has one brown eye and one blue, just like his rock star namesake, David Bowie.

Jo, of Taunton, Somerset, said: 'It needed cleaning, but was otherwise OK. Hester had a very guilty look on her face.'

Vet Tim said: 'This was highly unusual.'

THE CAT BURGLAR

A PECKISH pussy is in the moghouse after being exposed as a cunning cat burglar.

Thieving tabby Dillon learned how to tug his owners' fridge door open with a paw so he could nick food.

Baffled Julie Fisher and partner Simon Jordan could not understand when fish, sausages, chicken and even a packet of wine gums vanished.

The pair even suspected each other of secretly snacking. But one day Julie, 29, found the fridge door ajar – and the penny dropped.

She fitted it with a child lock to thwart Dillon. But the undaunted puss just switched to raiding neighbours' homes.

He was seen making off along next door's garden path with a whole fish in his mouth.

Julie, of Wimbledon, south-west London, said: 'He just left the fridge door open behind him. Now our neighbour has put a lock on as well!'

Julie, who has had Dillon for three years, added: 'For months we wondered where all the food from the fridge was going.'

Accountant Simon, 38, said: 'We couldn't understand how he was piling on weight – now we know.'

Animal expert Dr Roger Mugford said: 'Cats are very manipulative and clever. They have a tremendous sense of smell and if there is food to be had they will try to reach it.'

CAT LITTER

SHADOW the moggie is driving his owners clean out of their minds by bringing them LITTER as love tokens.

The three-year-old black cat turned street-sweeper when his family moved into a new detached house on a posh estate.

He started hauling old cigarette packets, dog-ends, chip wrappers and crisp bags through his cat flap and dumping them all over the £150,000 home.

Shadow's biggest 'trophies' so far are a 4-foot length of bubble wrap and a bin liner.

Owner Graham King, 50, said: 'The whole neighbour-hood's spotless, but our house is strewn with Shadow's rubbish.

'We thought he was just out of sorts when we moved, and expected him to get out of the habit. But instead he got worse. His favourite trick is to wake us up at night after dragging another load of rubbish into our bedroom. Most owners get upset when their cats bring home birds and mice but we'd be delighted – it'd make a nice change.'

Shadow's weird behaviour has bewildered public relations consultant Graham, his 47-year-old wife Tricia and their children.

And top animal psychologist Dr Roger Mugford is also baffled. He said: 'This is amazing. I've never heard of anything like it. I'd love to meet this cat. If a dog was collecting litter I could have explained it away as some form of nest-building compulsion. But cats simply don't have that instinct. I suppose it's possible that he could have been unsettled by the recent house move – but I've never heard of this kind of response before.'

Graham's son Tim said: 'Shadow's just eccentric – he's doing his bit to keep Britain tidy.'

CAT BURGLAR

A STRAY cat repaid the pet-lover who rescued her from an animal sanctuary by nicking him clothes from washing lines and a launderette.

Moggie Thomasina has dragged in 80 tea towels, a dressing gown, an Arsenal FC shirt, and dozens of socks and knickers for Kit Gittins, 65.

Kit, of Bedford, said: 'It's her way of showing her love. We collect the clothes in a plastic bag and return them to the owners.'

THIEF JASPER IS CAT IT AGAIN

A FAMILY are being tormented by a real cat burglar – their moggie Jasper.

Owner Della Curtis had to move house after her pet plagued neighbours with his night-time raids.

Now the Burmese tom is at it again – stealing baubles and chocolates from Sarah Martin's Christmas tree across the road.

Sarah, 25, who has two cats of her own, put in a magnetic cat flap. But Jasper still smashed his way in.

Della, 54, of Bidford-on-Avon, Warwickshire, said: 'It's a bit embarrassing.'

CHAPTER 4

LIKE LAZAR-PUSS: MOGGIES THAT CAME BACK FROM THE DEAD

HUMP BACK

JOHN Major's runaway moggie Humphrey is back at 10 Downing Street, just 24 hours after he was declared 'missing, presumed dead.'

The Premier had feared the seven-year-old black-and-white mouser, who ran away from Number 10 three weeks ago, had died of a kidney complaint.

But squaddies at the Royal Army Medical College in Pimlico, half a mile from Westminster, rang the PM to say: 'We've got your cat!'

They only realised the moggie they had adopted belonged to Number 10 when they read reports of his suspected death.

A Downing Street driver was sent to bring Humphrey home for a reunion with Mr Major. An aide confirmed: 'The PM is delighted Humphrey has returned.'

USED SMARTIE

A CAT that followed Julie Wilson-Hamilton home in Sturry, Kent, turned out to be Smartie, the moggie she lost two years ago. Now Julie wants to trace whoever has been caring for her pet since its disappearance.

LOST KITTY'S PEAK CLIMB

FUDGE the kitten wandered off from home and climbed to the top of one of Britain's highest mountains.

The six-month-old ginger tom was found soaking wet and barely alive at the summit of 2,593-foot Grisedale Pike in the Lake District.

An amazed hiker wrapped him in his jacket and carried him down.

Fudge was finally reunited with owner Wendy Shill, 44, who runs a hotel at the foot of the mountain. He climbed the peak in five hours.

Wendy said: 'We've dubbed him Top Cat. It's a difficult mountain to climb and I'm amazed he did it. We think he followed walkers up there.'

OUR MOGGIE IS BURY TIRED

STUNNED Pauline Bristowe found her cat asleep on a bed – after she thought she had buried him.

Pauline, 53, and husband Max, 54, had held a tearful funeral with their three daughters after a moggie was killed by a car.

They thought the black-and-white victim was their kitty Griffin.

But then Pauline, of Barnsley, South Yorkshire, found him sleeping on a duvet, and realised they had buried the wrong cat.

CAT ENDS FOUR-YEAR FLAP

STUNNED Helena Laughton was called by a vet to say he had found her cat – four years after it went missing.

The black moggie ran off weeks after being given to student Helena on her 18th birthday.

Vets traced the cat to Helena from a microchip under its skin after finding it 15 miles away.

Helena, 22, from Horsham, West Sussex, said: 'He's my dream cat.'

CAT'S NOT MY PUSSY

A DISTRAUGHT gran who thought a cat hit by a car was her puss told a vet to put it to sleep – only to find her pet Bobby safe and well later.

Then Pauline Rogerson's neighbour David Stead claimed the late long-haired cat was HIS pet Satan. But Satan also turned up OK.

The puzzled pair are trying to trace the REAL owner. Pauline, 66, said: 'You couldn't make it up.'

The Abbey Vets' Clinic in Barnsley, South Yorkshire, said: 'It's all very confusing.'

ASH NOT MY CAT

SAD Rick Fuller spent £110 on a funeral for his cat, and was stunned when it turned up ALIVE weeks later.

Rick, 39, had gone to the vet's to identify a ginger tom killed by a car near his home.

Convinced that it was his beloved missing pet Whisky, he had the cat cremated and its ashes put in a mahogany urn.

The container – complete with special commemorative plaque – was given pride of place on the mantelpiece.

But Rick, a property manager from Farnborough, Hampshire, was baffled two weeks later when he spotted a photo of a lost Whisky in his local paper – with an appeal for the owner to come forward.

He said: 'I was convinced Whisky was a box of ashes on my mantelpiece. Yet there was a picture of him – and he looked right as rain. I couldn't believe my eyes – it was like seeing a ghost.'

Rick, who has had Whisky from a kitten, called the number in the paper and was reunited with his pet.

The three-year-old moggie had also been hit by a car, but had survived after treatment by a different vet and was handed over to the RSPCA.

Now Rick faces a dilemma over what to do with the ashes on his mantelpiece. He said: 'I've spent a small fortune giving a stranger's cat a decent send-off, so if someone nearby has lost a ginger tom they can have the ashes.

'It's great to have Whisky back and he's happy to be home. I just have someone else's dead cat in my house.'

MOGGIE'S FIVE-YEAR JAUNT

A CAT missing for five years has been reunited with his owners after they saw him in an animal sanctuary magazine.

Black moggie Bullet vanished from the home of Steve and Diana Dent in Eastgate, County Durham.

He first got his name when they took him in after their children found him with gun-inflicted wounds.

But a year later Bullet went missing. Stunned Steve, 41, saw him in the magazine – and the cat has now arrived home. Steve said: 'It's a dream come true.'

'MIRACLE' MOGGIE

MISSING cat Timmy stunned owner Will Massingale by turning up at his OWN funeral.

Sports instructor Will, 23, was burying what he thought was his puss after the cat had been killed by a car outside his home.

But when Timmy wandered into the garden, Will realised the dead moggie was a lookalike belonging to a neighbour.

Will, of Bude, Cornwall, said: 'I thought I was hallucinating.'

CAT'S TWO LATE BACK

RELIEVED Katherine McAllister was reunited with her runaway cat just days after buying another kitten to replace her.

Muffin disappeared from mum-of-five Katherine's home in Bridge of Don, Aberdeen.

A month later she bought kitten Moggie, but then discovered that Muffin had been found 150 miles away in Glasgow.

Katherine, 47, said: 'She's back, but she's not very fond of the kitten. I think she's jealous.'

CAT FOUND SIX YEARS ON

TOMCAT Colin has been reunited with his owner after going missing SIX YEARS ago.

The ginger moggie vanished from Emma Phillips' home in Barkingside, Essex, in 1999.

Colin is believed to have lived as a stray in the town until a woman who had been feeding the cat for a few months handed him to pet rescue charity, PDSA.

A vet found a microchip in the scruff of the puss's neck and phoned delighted mum-of-two Emma, 34.

She recognised 13-year-old Colin immediately. She said: 'He had a rip in his ear and black dots on his face.'

CHAPTER 5

LOVIN' FELINE: CATS WITH UNUSUAL CHUMS

THE BEAST OF FRIENDS

OLIVER the budgie and Bee Bee the cat are such purr-fect pals they even eat supper together.

In any normal house the tiny bird would give the 14-year-old tabby tom a wide berth.

But owner Gaynor Barton said yesterday: 'Bee Bee has never so much as raised a claw in anger. And Oliver is just as happy in the company of the cat.'

Oliver and Bee Bee hit it off the moment the blue budgie arrived as a six-week-old chick.

Mum-of-two Gaynor, 42, of Blaby, Leicestershire, added: 'Bee Bee was scared of birds after being set upon by a furious blackbird. So he was just as wary of Oliver as the budgie was of him. When I started letting Oliver out of his cage Bee Bee ignored him – he's such a placid cat – and Oliver's courage grew. As soon as they both realised that neither was a threat they started getting on famously. Now I can leave them alone together and come back to find them sitting side by side, watching the world go by out of the window.

'Oliver loves biscuits and eats them from my hand.

When I say, "Give Bee Bee one", he chucks it over at the cat. He will also give Bee Bee a peck when I say, "Give the pussycat a kiss", and he pecks at cat food in Bee Bee's bowl.'

School helper Gaynor, who lives with hubby Richard, 44, and children Karen, 15, and Paul, 21, added: 'I don't know what Tom and Jerry would make of it, but I think it's lovely.'

A spokesman for the Royal Society for the Protection of Birds said: 'It may be that the cat does not think of the budgie as a bird at all. They probably just see each other as mates.'

MOGGIE'S MOUSEMATE

A MOUSE called Mickey has struck up an amazing friendship . . . with a CAT.

The rodent was being treated for shock at Oxford Animal Hospital, in a cage near pregnant moggie Emma.

After she gave birth to three kittens, he burrowed out, squeezed between their bars and joined them.

Vet Keeley Foley said: 'We couldn't believe it when we came in the next morning and found Mickey suckling on Emma along with all the kittens. Now Mickey runs around the cage, curls up with the kittens and even sits on Emma's head or between her paws. The cat loves the mouse and the mouse loves the cat. It's not exactly in the true traditions of Tom and Jerry.'

But Keeley warned that three-year-old Emma, who needed an emergency Caesarean, might not be so friendly once her mothering instincts subsided.

So she is being returned to her owners along with her kittens, while six-month-old Mickey will need a new home.

But at least he lived to tell the tail.

PUSS 'N' BEAUTS

A KITTEN is feline fine after befriending a couple of ducks.

It was a purr-fect day for the tabby and his two duckling friends as they were whiskered off to play together for the first time.

The fun started at Burlorne Pillow Farm in Bodmin, Cornwall, on the puss's first day away from his mum.

Thankfully the two ducklings – both India Runners – avoided a cat-astrophe.

The moggie was having so much fun with his daffy mates that he forgot that cats normally like a spot of duck for dinner.

It looks like the trio are shaping up to be furry good friends. We just hope their relationship doesn't quack up.

CHAPTER 6

SUPAW HEROES: CATS WITH A LOTTA BOTTLE

ROAD RESCUE HERO GIZZY IS TOP CAT

GIZZY the cat rescued another puss hit by a car by grabbing the injured animal in its jaws and carrying it from the busy road to safety.

The tabby tom even performed first aid on his neighbour's kitten by licking its wounds.

Brave Gizzy was named 'Hero Cat of the Year' in a nationwide contest run by *Your Cat* magazine.

His prize is a year's supply of cat food and a trip to Egypt for owners Adele and Alex Murdoch.

Factory worker Adele, 32, of Stevenston, Ayrshire, said: 'Our neighbour told us about the rescue when we returned from holiday. I didn't think cats did that sort of thing.'

CAT SAVES FIVE KITTENS FROM INFERNO

A COURAGEOUS cat who ran five times into a blazing building to save her kittens has won the hearts of millions.

Firemen told how the stray, scorched and burned, braved the inferno again and again.

After bringing her brood out one by one, she carried them to safety across the street.

Then, with her eyes blistered shut so she could not see, she touched each kitten with her nose to count they were all there.

Rescuers in Brooklyn, New York, who took the family to an animal sanctuary, nicknamed the mum Scarlet because of her red raw burns.

And after her story appeared in newspapers, more than 700 people offered the cats a home.

Shelter manager Marge Stein said: 'She's a wonderful animal who did a courageous thing. Even with animals, there's no way of measuring a mother's love.'

Vets believe Scarlet will recover her sight and say the four-week-old kittens are recovering well.

CAT SAVES PAIR FROM BLAZE HELL

A SLEEPING couple were saved from a blaze at their home when their cat sounded an alarm.

John Jenkins, 60, and wife Edna, 53, were alerted when Micha rang the battery-powered bell he uses to signal that he wants to go out.

The fire was heading for the couple's home in Penicuik, Midlothian, after ripping through a garden shed and spreading to a garage.

Pianist John said: 'If it wasn't for Micha my wife and I might not be here right now.'

SICK MOGGIE TAKES HIMSELF TO VET

A BADLY injured moggie saved his life by going to a vet on HIS OWN.

Staff were stunned when the stray, who could barely breathe, wandered into the surgery, sat down and refused to budge.

An X-ray revealed the eight-year-old cat – dubbed Ricky – had a ruptured diaphragm.

Vet Patrick Liversage carried out a life-saving op at his practice in Little Clacton, Essex, and Ricky is now making a good recovery.

Animal aid worker Angie Harris is caring for Ricky, who is thought to have been run over by a car.

She said: 'It's amazing he was able to take himself to the vet. He is a remarkable cat.'

PYTHON ATE HERO PUSSSSSSS

A PLUCKY puss died a hero, saving her sleeping owners from a deadly python.

The 7-foot snake, which had escaped from a pet shop, slipped into the family's flat through an open window.

Pepita the family cat blocked the snake's path and miaowed a warning at the top of her voice.

The noise woke her owners and their three kids, aged four to nine.

The terrified family managed to escape ... just as the python swallowed their beloved moggie at home in Valencia, Spain.

LONG ARM OF THE PAW

BRAVE Bonnie the cat foiled a raid at her owner's warehouse and sent two robbers fleeing covered in blood.

The amazing moggie tore into the crooks with her teeth and claws after they broke in at night.

Bonnie, a six-year-old tortoiseshell, spotted them as she prowled in search of mice. The men were trying to steal tons of pet food from the building belonging to Mike Powell.

He said: 'Bonnie's a real beauty and worth her weight in gold. You don't need a guard dog with a tiger like her about. Once the gang got inside they could have cleared the place, but Bonnie had other ideas. They had only managed to load a few bags of dog food into their lorry when she launched herself into action.'

Mike, 38, of Swadlincote, Derbyshire, added: 'We found her next day cowering and sore, with fur everywhere, but you could see from the scene that the intruders had it much worse.'

Police discovered two types of human blood and hope it will help them nail the raiders. A spokesman said: 'The warehouse could have been cleared if the cat hadn't been there.'

MOGGIE SAVES BABY BIRDS

THREE tiny birds cheated death by a whisker when they were rescued by a CAT.

The baby song thrushes looked doomed when Jerry the moggie found them lying helplessly on a lawn.

But he ignored his natural instincts and raised the alarm by miaowing loudly.

His cries woke owner Anne Shewring, 45, who dashed outside and found 12-year-old Jerry standing guard over the fledglings.

Anne, of Cirencester, Gloucestershire, said: 'Most cats would have eaten them but Jerry's a big softie. He's not into killing things.'

Anne took the birds to a sanctuary.

CHAPTER 7

FAT CATS: AND OTHER EXTREME MOGGIES

GREEN AND BEAR IT

A CAT has stunned vets by giving birth to a kitten with bright green fur. The rest of the litter in Copenhagen, Denmark, is perfectly normal.

TAB OF LARD

GIANT puss Thomas is more of a TUBBY than a tabby.

The ten-year-old is one of Britain's fattest cats at 28lb – scoffing four huge meals a day.

Owner Gladys Jarvis, 69, of Banbury, Oxfordshire, said: 'I've tried him on a diet, but he's having none of it.'

Thomas just pips 11-year-old tabby Casper who weighs 24lb. Owner Angela Rogers, 39, of Swansea, South Wales, said: 'He eats as much as a child.'

And bulging Barney, 12, who belongs to Kathleen Lee, 55, of Porton, Staffordshire, also weighs 24lb.

MOGZILLA

MEET Zac . . . Britain's mightiest moggie, weighing in at a whopping 2 stone.

The giant ginger tom, four times bigger than the average feline, ballooned in size after years of lapping up his favourite minced lamb.

And he piled on extra pounds scoffing shrimps, salmon and full-fat milk. Owner Neville King, 65, put 12-year-old Zac on a diet, but gave in when he SULKED.

Neville, of York, said: 'Zac is simply a cat who loves his food. He'll eat almost anything. He lets you know when he fancies a bite by hanging around you and making a nuisance of himself. We just feed him whenever he's hungry.'

Retired college lecturer Neville looks after 34lb Zac with his wife Ann. He said: 'His size does restrict him a bit. He doesn't climb trees or chase birds any more. But why should he? He can get all he wants to eat here.'

The fattest-ever cat was a 46lb tom named Himmy, who died in Queensland, Australia, in 1986.

PUSSY GALORE

MIAOW about that! Snowbie the cat has been named the longest pet moggie in the world.

The six-year-old measures a massive 3 foot 4 inches

from nose to tail. He has been entered in the book of *Guinness World Records*.

Owner Lorna Sutherland, 27, of Ellon, Aberdeenshire, who got him as a kitten, said Snowbie was once mistaken for a panther.

She added: 'He loves to sleep on my bed at night and particularly likes to lie at my feet. But this does tend to stop the flow of blood at times.'

SMOKEY'S A SPARKY OLD PUSS AT 32

BRITAIN'S oldest cat was feline fine yesterday after beating a string of setbacks to reach the age of 32.

Smokey's birthday makes her over 200 in cat years, but she tucked into a cake and a huge tin of her favourite food like a greedy kitten.

And Smokey had an extra reason to be happy – she has just been given a new home.

She was made homeless a year ago when her elderly owner died.

The moggie was half-DEAF, BLIND in one eye and on DRUGS for kidney trouble. She was even shot in the leg by a thug with an air gun.

But the plucky puss thrived after being taken in by the Cats Protection League in Cinderford, Gloucestershire. Smokey now lives with a widow in an idyllic cottage in nearby Stroud.

CPL worker Sara Cox, 48, said Smokey still has a vast appetite and goes for daily walks.

Sara added: 'Her lungs are certainly working well because she miaows loud enough. She is a tough old cookie.'

The world's oldest cat was tabby Puss, of Collumpton, Devon, who died aged 36 in 1939.

FAT CAT IN DOGHOUSE

A MONSTER moggie has to live in a DOG kennel because he is too fat to fit through a cat flap.

Lou weighs 15lb and his stomach scrapes the ground when he walks.

Staff at an animal sanctuary have had to house him in a 3-foot kennel. One worker said: 'Its door is twice as big as a cat flap.'

Lou was dumped by his owner because of high food bills. She told Blue Cross sanctuary chiefs she didn't think his size was linked to the large amount he ate.

Vets in Thirsk, North Yorkshire, are now trying to halve the tabby's weight to prevent a heart attack.

FIDGET'S NO WIDGET

MUNCHING moggie Fidget is twice the size of other cats having been given the free run of the pet shop where he lives.

Fidget, who was dumped at the store 13 years ago as a year-old kitten, even gets to open bags of food when he feels like a nibble, and now weighs 18lb.

Owner Wendy Kirk, 39, admitted: 'He's the fat-cat boss of this shop. If we aren't here he tears open a bag of his favourite.'

Wendy, whose hubby Shaun, 40, owns Pet Fare in North Shields, North Tyneside, added: 'It's no wonder he's as big as he is. But at least he's happy.'

TUBBY CAT

TOMMY the tabby is Britain's fattest cat – at 35lbs.

The ten-year-old pet used to scoff a bowl of chicken or porridge for breakfast, fish fingers or salmon at lunch and more chicken for supper.

But Tommy's owners Duncan and Lynne Watson, of Mansfield, Nottinghamshire, have now put him on a diet amid health fears.

Engineer Duncan said: 'He's always liked his grub.'

FURLESS KITTEN'S NOT FELINE THE CHILL

A TINY kitten born with NO fur is keeping warm by wearing jumpers knitted by her vet.

Animal sanctuary bosses are baffled why five-month-old moggie Freya can't grow fur, but vet Vicky Balbontin stepped in to help Freya beat the winter chill with Arran wool sweaters.

Vicky, a volunteer at the sanctuary, revealed: 'I knew she would be at risk from hypothermia. Young cats can die from the cold very easily. As she has grown I have knitted more, but I think she now needs a few new ones because they keep getting dirty.'

Kate Robinson, who runs the Willows Animal Sanctuary in New Pitsligo, Aberdeenshire, added: 'It's a mystery why she has no fur. Vicky decided Freya needed something to make sure she didn't get cold. She enjoys knitting, so she made some jackets and sweaters.'

DAVID MIAOWIE

A CAT has a real face oddity – one brown eye and one blue, like rock star David Bowie.

Space Oddity star Bowie, 56, damaged the pupil of his left eye in a fight at school. But Siamese cat Queeny, from Bangalore, India, has perfect vision.

THE MONSTER MOGGIE

A MYSTERIOUS big cat dubbed the Beast of Dartmoor has been unmasked ... as a 2-stone monster moggie named Sebastian.

Nervous locals in the Devon village of East Ogwell reported several recent sightings of a 2 feet 6 inch-high panther-like creature prowling surrounding fields.

But retired teacher Mike Healy, 66, revealed his puss was to blame. He said: 'A neighbour showed me a local paper story on the Beast and I just knew it was Sebastian. He IS bigger than the average cat and slinks around like a Wild West gunslinger. But the only time he's a danger is when he lies on you.'

He added: 'He's a big softie and wouldn't hurt anyone.'

PINK PANTHER

MOGGIE Brumas is at the centre of a hue-dunnit mystery, – after her coat suddenly turned from white to PINK.

Joan Worth, who owns the nine-year-old puss in Bratton Clovelly, Devon, said: 'We have no idea why it happened.'

CHAPTER 8

PUSSIN' BRUTES: WHEN MOGGIES GO BAD

MEW AH CAT-ONA

A CAT named Eric Cantona loves to go on the attack and keeps MAULING the postman.

The pet ambushes the postie in the garden or bites and scratches his fingers as he puts letters through owner Mike Leach's letter box.

Now mail bosses have warned Manchester United fan Mike that his deliveries could be stopped unless he gives the mad moggie the red card.

Barman Mike, 24, said: 'He is a bit on the wild side and lies in wait for the postman. He goes for the hands, but then calms down, picks the letters up in his mouth and brings them to me.'

Mike, who lives with his mother Pat in Rhyl, North Wales, named the cat Cantona because he can be moody and unpredictable – like United's former striker.

Mike added: 'He has certainly picked up some of Eric's fiery ways. He is fine with me, but will go for anybody else – even mum.'

Sorting office chief Paul Quinn said: 'It is not amusing. The postman's hands have been badly scratched and there is a risk of infection. We need to work out how this can be stopped – maybe by a wire cage round the letter box.'

PASSION KILLER

MAN-hating moggie Flo is wrecking her owner's love life by savaging every fella who comes to the house.

Veterinary nurse Louise Anderssen-Matthews, 26, hasn't had a passionate night at home for more than a year because of the fearsome feline.

She said: 'When a man walks in, Flo's back arches. She starts hissing and spitting and flies at them. She sinks her claws into their legs and they run for their lives. I dread the thought of trying to smuggle a man in past her. She was lovely as a kitten, but she has grown into a monster.'

Desperate Louise, of Newport, Isle of Wight, has bought several pairs of Wellington boots in different sizes to protect fellas' legs.

She became so worried that she contacted the Channel 4 programme *Absolutely Animals* for advice and sent them a video of Flo attacking her friends.

They sent a pet psychiatrist to study Flo and to advise how best to calm her homicidal attitude to men.

Louise, who bought Flo 14 months ago when she was nine weeks old, said: 'When she was young she was very playful and just like any other kitten. I first noticed a change in her behaviour after leaving her with a male lodger for a few weeks when she was six months old. If you looked at her she would get very agitated. She is OK with women, but one look from a man and she goes berserk.'

Louise added: 'It puts men off from calling here – I haven't had a boyfriend for 14 months.'

RESERVOIR MOG

POSTIES refuse to deliver letters to Kathy Simmonds' house in case they are mauled by her psycho moggie.

The bloodthirsty chocolate Burmese cat, called Rummy, has already savaged THREE of them.

Kathy's mail is now left with neighbours. And other attacks on the milkman, dustman and passers-by have forced mum-of-two Kathy, 40, to keep her eight-year-old puss indoors.

She said: 'We couldn't believe it when a note came through the door saying, "Unable to deliver mail, threatened by cat."'

Neighbour Nick Toone, 38, said: 'He's a nightmare. He lies in wait and jumps out. He spits at you and worries the kids. If you ask me he should be muzzled.'

Kathy and engineer husband Bob, 41, live in Bognor Regis, West Sussex, with children Kayleigh, seven, and David, 23 months – and a three-year-old hamster called Ford Escort.

She added: 'Rummy is terrified of our toddler and

hamster and is well behaved inside the house. But as soon as the door opens he becomes a wild thing outside.'

The Royal Mail said three staff were left with claw marks in their legs and one female postie needed hospital treatment for a deep wound.

MICE WORK, MOLLIE

MOLLIE the cat – who caught 2,000 mice a year – has been buried with a 'simply the best' medal and a stuffed toy mouse in Mayfield, East Sussex.

KILLER CATS WIPE OUT 275 MILLION

CATS kill up to 275 million other animals and birds in Britain each year, a new report says.

Mice are their most common victim, followed by voles and shrews. Declining species like house sparrows and dormice are under particular threat, said the study by the Mammal Society.

And cats often kill for kicks, spending 30 minutes playing with their prey – then leaving it.

A study of 1,000 moggies over five months found they killed 4,000 mice, 2,000 voles and 2,000 shrews. Only 162 rats died – probably because they are more likely to fight back.

Sparrows topped the list of killed birds, while frogs and squirrels also fell victim.

There are nine million pet cats in the UK and the report suggests each kills 33 times a year.

Society chairman Professor Stephen Harris said: 'Cats can be a serious problem for wildlife.'

BBC GIVE PET PUSS THE BOOT

BBC bosses are giving their pet puss the boot for scratching a worker after the woman made an official complaint that Mac had 'savaged' her legs.

Chiefs ruled he must go, and will send him to a rescue centre next week if he is not re-homed.

An internal email says: 'Mac made an unprovoked attack on a member of staff resulting in significant injuries to the person's feet and ankles.'

Another says the moggie is 'a danger'.

But some staff at the translation centre in Caversham, Berkshire, fear he will be put down, and are fighting to save him.

They adopted the black-and-white stray as their mouser in 1996, and have even made him a security pass.

One employee joked: 'He just lounges around on sofas like all BBC fat cats.'

But a Beeb official said: 'We can't take the risk.'

CAT SAVAGES POSTIE

MAIL chiefs are threatening to stop deliveries to a Cardiff flat after postie John Blackburn was mauled three times by a cat.

Hissing moggie Boo Boo leaps up and claws John as he shoves mail through the letter box.

John, 57, said: 'The last scratch was quite deep. Blood was dripping on to the driveway and over letters in my bag. The cat jumped up on the window sill and looked out as if to say, "Got you."'

Boo Boo's owner John Davies, 62, said: 'She's just playful. I'll have to call her Boo Boo the Barbarian.'

He may rig up a mesh mailbox inside his door to foil the cat.

CAT SAVAGES CAT BURGLAR

A CAT burglar was sent packing by a family CAT.

Elderly, one-eyed tortoiseshell Mitmo savaged the thief despite having just three teeth.

The moggie had been lying on owner Denise Carter's bed when they heard late night noises and went downstairs to investigate.

Denise, 33, said: 'A burglar was trying to put his arm through the window and Mitmo just launched herself at him. He tried to shake her off, but she would not let go.

She was hissing and spitting as she dug her teeth and claws deeper.'

The bloodied crook fled after banging 12-year-old Mitmo against a wall in Southampton.

Denise and hubby Paul bought the pet for daughter Kirstie, 11. Mitmo was recovering after 'a few cuddles'.

Denise said: 'She's very territorial.'

DEVIL MOG

TERRIFIED postmen are refusing to deliver mail to a pensioner's home because they are frightened of his ferocious CAT.

Moggie Purrdey, 11, leaps at posties like a tiger and then mauls them, drawing blood with his claws.

And that's despite being kept on a leash in the garden by owner Alan Rice. Staff have now sent Mr Rice an official note saying they can no longer give him his mail.

A postwoman who was attacked put a sticker on one of his letters saying: 'Unable to deliver, dog at large' – with a line through a drawing of a dog and the word 'cat' inserted.

Mr Rice, 79, of New Milton, Hampshire, said: 'The Royal Mail don't seem to be very keen on Purrdey. Apparently there's a warning notice up in the local sorting office saying "Beware of Alan Rice's cat". It's embarrassing. I think of Purrdey as a lovely old fellow. I was aware of an incident when he spat at a postman, but I thought he'd been behaving himself.'

Mr Rice, who sits on Hampshire County Council, had hoped the leash would help protect posties.

But Royal Mail spokesman Adrian Booth said: 'This cat is dangerous. He believes he's a tiger and lands on people, digging his claws in as deeply as possible. Six or seven of our staff have been attacked. They should not be subjected to this.'

SASCHA THE SLASHER

A COUNCIL put a fluffy KITTEN on its 'violent animals' database after a building inspector suffered a tiny scratch.

The man was supervising repairs to charity worker Brian Jackson's home when four-month-old Sascha hopped on to his shoulder.

Brian, 55, said: 'He screamed and terrified the poor kitten. She was only small so she dug her claws in to hold on.'

Brian, of Colne, Lancaster, then got a letter from Pendle Council telling him that due to the 'attack' his address had been put on a database listing dangerous pets.

The move was particularly potty as Sascha is NOT Brian's moggie. She belongs to neighbour Dirk Kriete, though she often pops next door.

Brian blasted the council for wasting time and money

Pink Panther: it is a question of hue-dunnit for the owners of moggie
Brumas after the kitty's coat miraculously turned from white to pink.

Nervous postmen refused to deliver letters to Alan Rice after his mental moggie Purrdey attacked a series of Royal Mail workers – leaping at them, mauling them and drawing blood.

Above: Vicious mouser Purrdey gazes through his owner's letterbox.

Above: Four-month-old kitten Sascha earned herself the nickname 'Sascha the Slasher' after she was put on a council's 'violent animals' database when a building inspector got on the wrong side of the little kitten and received a tiny scratch.

Above: Danger cat Bat terrorised postmen so much that they refused to deliver the mail. The psycho puss would sit under his cat flap waiting to swipe at unwitting posties.

Right: Miracle moggie Sooty with her owner's daughter, 18-year-old Claire Mountford-Davies, who found the adventurous puss after she undertook a moggiethon, trekking 100 miles from Bath to Swansea back to her former home.

Right: Thrill-seeking puss Maisy in the arms of her owner Rhys Lewis, nine. Maisy stowed away on a lorry to rejoin her owners in Jersey just three months after they left her 700 miles away in France.

Below: Nine-year-old feline Sage pictured with web designer Stephen Park, who found his wife's mog trapped beside the engine of his Mazda after driving 30 miles to work from Ayrshire to Glasgow.

Left: Feline Bob became an Arsenal kit-ty after he crept onto the Arsenal team's bus at the Hertfordshire training ground and travelled 100 miles with the team to Birmingham.

Above: Joey the alcoholic mog got as pussed as a newt on Bacardi Breezers, lager and cider during secret binges at his local pub.

The purr-fect solution: Custard the Cat, who suffers from weak hind legs, gets in shape by doing the moggie paddle twice a week in a hydrotherapy pool built for dogs.

over the incident. He said: 'Snarling, bloodthirsty Dobermanns or pit bulls are violent – not a cute little kitten.'

The database is used by council workers to warn them of potential hazards when they visit homes.

DANGER CAT BAT MAIMS POSTMAN PAT

TERRIFIED postmen are refusing to deliver mail to a house because they are scared of a dangerous CAT.

They say their hands are being ripped to shreds by ginger tom Bat as they shove post through the cat flap. The posties also claim the six-year-old moggie claws their legs with vicious swipes.

Now bosses have sent owner Dan Coyne a letter saying deliveries are suspended because of the 'guard cat'.

Stunned Dan, 23, said: 'I can't believe they are scared of him.' But the sales manager did admit: 'Bat is a bit of a psycho and has been known to launch himself at people. He gets very wound up by the postman and sits under the cat flap waiting for him. As the postie pushes the letters through, I've seen Bat try to swipe him with his claws. He was a rescue cat and is only little, but he does get stroppy.'

Dan, of Cranbrook, Kent, has been told to collect his own post until he takes action to control Bat.

The Royal Mail letter said: 'The postmen are experiencing

problems with your Guard Cat. It sounds ridiculous, I know, but as they deliver through the flap the cat scratches them. More incredible than this, your cat has been known to jump on the postmen's legs and dig his claws in.'

Dan said he has a letter box, but posties used the flap because it was easier. He added: 'If they are that scared they should use the box. It is ridiculous.'

The Royal Mail said: 'Staff safety is paramount. We are discussing the possibility of a box on the gate.'

POSTIE IN CAT FLAP

A POSTWOMAN refuses to deliver to a house because Monty the moggie attacks her feet.

She claims the four-year-old ginger tom hides in the garden before pouncing.

But owner Mark Wheeler, 47, of Chippenham, Wiltshire, said: 'Monty is just being playful.'

CHAPTER 9

MYSTIC MOG: PSYCHIC PUSSIES

I'M FELINE LUCKY

PUNTER Brian Halter has his own phantom tipster – a dead cat.

Ghostly pet Marmy, who died two years ago, visits him before big races and gives him the winning horse's number by blowing in his ear.

Brian, 64, of Chepstow, Gwent, said: 'I've won thousands.' For the next Grand National, Marmy tips 10, 11, 3 and 4 – in that order.

CAT'S A CLAW-VOYANT

LOUIE the psychic cat gets a strange feline whenever diabetic owner Russell Howarth threatens to fall ill.

He miaows at the top of his voice to warn Russell it's time for one of his four daily insulin shots.

Russell, 41, said: 'He seems to have a sixth sense. Whenever he makes a racket and tears at the carpets, my blood sugar levels are always low. I don't know how or why Louie can do it, but he will follow me around howling until I take insulin.'

Wife Irene, 37, of Preston, Lancashire, claimed 12-year-old Louie has even saved Russell's life.

She said: 'Once Louie was playing merry hell and I found Russell unconscious. The doctor said he could have died within an hour if it wasn't for Louie.'

Local vet Neale Roach said: 'Louie is picking up on Russell's daily routine. Only animals can do this.'

CHAPTER 10

FUR, FUR AWAY: MOGGIES' INCREDIBLE JOURNEYS

PURRGEOT ESTATE

MISCHIEVOUS moggie Rufty lost at least one of her nine lives and her tail after a terror trip under a car bonnet.

The kitten had taken refuge from the rain by nestling up to the engine of owner Les Hazelgrave's motor. But cat-napping Rufty failed to bail out when shop manager Les set off on his 13-mile trip to work.

The injured cat only emerged when Les, 40, got back home near Oban, Scotland, nine hours later.

Les's newspaper editor wife Moira Kerr had been searching all day for the four-month-old black kitten.

Moira, 38, said: 'We have five cats and the other four had come in soaking wet, but there was no sign of Rufty. When Les arrived home at teatime, Rufty came in after him – bedraggled and covered in oil, but dry. That's when we realised what had happened. She was dry because she'd been in the engine.'

Vet Frankie Miller had to amputate Rufty's tail, which he reckoned must have got caught in a moving part.

Rufty also needed stitches in deep cuts on three paws, but the ordeal doesn't seem to have affected her much.

PUSS IN BOATS

A STOWAWAY moggie nicknamed Roughneck has been caught and flown to Aberdeen after hitching a lift on a supply ship to an oil platform in the middle of the North Sea.

WHISKER YOU WERE HERE

A CAT that disappeared from its Madrid home turned up 11 days later in the village where its owners holiday each year – 250 miles away.

HOLS GAFFE AS MOGGIE IS PACKED

SHOCKED Clara Kent opened her suitcase on holiday – and found she had packed her CAT.

Black-and-white moggie Tessa had crept into the case after Clara left the lid open while packing.

Hubby Lester later shut it, and the tom was only freed TEN HOURS later after a 250-MILE trip.

Clara, 69, said: 'I got the fright of my life when he popped out.'

Lester put the case in their car boot at Mells, Suffolk, at 6.15 a.m.

The couple drove 20 miles and caught a coach to Builth Wells, Wales.

After they arrived at the Greyhound Hotel at 4.30 p.m., Clara started unpacking – and out leapt ten-month-old Tessa.

Clara said: 'It's incredible our cat didn't suffocate.'

Lester said: 'I noticed my case was heavy.'

The hotel let Tessa stay in the Kents' bathroom for their two-night break.

MOGGIETHON CAT WALKS 100 MILES

A BLACK cat called Sooty trekked an amazing 100 miles back to her old home after her owner moved house.

The miracle moggie's incredible journey between Bath and Swansea took SIX MONTHS.

She was found hungry, bedraggled and miaowing by the 18-year-old daughter of her owner, Reverend Jennifer Mountford-Davies, who lives near her mum's former house.

Jennifer, 47, said: 'I'm amazed. Sooty was very skinny and exhausted. Her long hair was matted and filthy. We are wondering how she got over the Severn Bridge!'

Five-year-old Sooty vanished a month after Jennifer took a post as minister of the United Reformed Churches in Rush Hill and Larkhall, Bath.

Jennifer and trucker husband Gordon, 52, moved with Sooty and their other two cats, but daughter Claire and her brother Jonathan, 20, stayed in Swansea to rent a flat.

Jennifer said: 'Sooty missed them. They were always treating her to chocolate. We feared she'd got lost, or been run over.'

Music student Claire added: 'We thought we'd never see her again. But she's shown an amazing sixth sense.'

RSPCA superintendent Kevin Manning said: 'Cats sometimes go on long journeys back to the places and people where they were most happy.'

TIGGER'S CATWALK

THREE-legged cat Tigger, who moved three miles with his owners to a new home, has trekked back 76 times in Freshwater, Isle of Wight.

CAT TURNS UP 200 MILES AWAY ON TV

DELIGHTED Mandy Cannon was reunited with her lost cat after spotting him 200 miles away on TV.

Mandy, 37, saw tabby Tigger on Channel 4's *Pet Rescue* show three months after he vanished from her home in Witley, Surrey.

He was having a leg amputated after being run over . . . in BRISTOL.

CAT'S IN TRANSIT

EBONY the cat is recovering after surviving a 170-mile ride under the bonnet of a van.

She chose the engine bay of Mo Yussuf's Transit for a doze as he visited his sister Regina. And when Mo, 42, started the motor, the sleepy black moggie was too scared to flee.

Ebony, pet of Regina's neighbours Brett and Sharon Mackenzie in Great Yarmouth, Norfolk, clung on grimly as clothing buyer Mo drove ten miles to visit friends, then 130 miles back home to Stepney, East London.

She crouched on a shelf in the engine overnight, then endured another 30-mile trip round London.

Terrified Ebony was finally discovered when Mo's colleague Jim Dear, 50, lifted the bonnet to check the oil. After failing to tempt her out with milk and chicken, the two pals called in RSPCA inspector Roy Blackburn, who jacked up the van and dragged her out by the tail.

Roy said: 'She's quite fat, and was well and truly stuck.'

Luckily, four-year-old Ebony's home phone number was on her collar and she was reunited next day with her relieved owners – unharmed except for a few oil smears.

Graphic designer Brett, 28, said: 'It's incredible to think she went such a distance. We thought we had lost her for ever.'

Mo said: 'I had no idea she was in the engine. It's just lucky that Jim checked the oil.'

CAT STRAYS 50 MILES

A BLACK cat who went missing is home safe and sound after being found 50 MILES away.

Jack strayed from Ashby de la Zouch, Leicestershire, five months ago. Owners Will Evans, 34, and Lisa Garley, 32, had given up hope of seeing him again.

But RSPCA officials found the moggie in Mansfield, Nottinghamshire, and were able to trace the pair thanks to an ID chip they had fitted to their pet.

Lisa said: 'He must have hitched a lift. He likes getting into cars.'

MOGGIE'S 620-MILE CATNAP

BILLY the cat is in purr-fect health, despite a terrifying 620-mile truck journey.

The moggie had crept into the back of a Newcastle-based pick-up for a nap. But driver Martin Spiers, 26, did not see him and set off on a 36-hour trip delivering skylights in Glasgow, Manchester, Wales and Shrewsbury.

The black cat was apparently too scared to move until he was finally seen climbing into the ENGINE.

Martin recognised the cat and returned him to neighbour Jeanette Hogg.

She said: 'I can't believe this happened. Thank God they found Billy and knew where he came from.'

Martin said: 'I think Billy must have climbed under the cover on the back of my vehicle because of the bad weather up north. As soon as I saw him I recognised him as the neighbour's pet.'

MY ENGINE'S PURRING

TRUCKER Jack Harrison drove 300 miles up the motorway with a black cat under his bonnet.

Two-year-old puss Penny clung on for one of her nine lives as Jack, 43, left Brighton at 4 a.m. bound for Holyhead, North Wales. Jack discovered Penny, who had clambered under the truck's bonnet to avoid the rain, when he stopped in Cheshire.

He said: 'I jacked up the cab and saw her two big, round, yellow eyes.'

After leaving her in Holyhead, Jack took a ferry to Ireland and picked the cat up on the way back before returning her to her owners – his neighbours Paul and Sophie Chambers.

MUMMY RETURNS

ESTHER the cat trekked ten miles to her old home in Cowling, West Yorkshire, and gave birth to three kittens in the garden.

VAN RADIO IS SO PURR

A VAN driver thought his radio was playing up when he heard squeaking for a week – until a thirsty CAT sprang out of his dashboard.

Antiques dealer Rodney Dodson, 54, drove hundreds of miles before he discovered the black-and-white moggie.

Rodney, of Waterlooville, Hampshire, said: 'I couldn't believe it when she suddenly appeared.'

He thinks the cat climbed into his Volkswagen while it was parked.

PUSS TREKS 700 MILES TO JOIN OWNERS

MAISY the cat stowed away on a lorry to rejoin her owners – three months after they left her 700 miles away in France.

Anthony Lewis and wife Sam gave their moggie to the buyers of their home because they did not want to put her through the upheaval of moving to Jersey.

But they were amazed when Maisy then turned up in the van delivering some of their belongings to their new abode in the Channel Islands.

She had sneaked aboard the truck and gone without food or water for two days as it travelled across France.

Her journey began in the Languedoc region near Spain and ended with a ferry trip to Jersey.

Delivery driver Tim Morley, 44, said: 'I loaded the van up in the middle of the night and when I got to Jersey I left it in the depot overnight. When I went back I could hear faint crying from the van and saw the cat. I put food down and she came out. Then I rang Anthony and described the cat. He said it sounded just like Maisy.'

Journalist Anthony, 34, who had been running a gîte complex in France, said: 'We were overjoyed. We always knew she was a clever cat. We really didn't think we'd see her again, but we're glad she's back.'

But Maisy faced a last hurdle before starting a new life with Anthony, Sam and their son Rhys, nine.

Immigration officials declared she had to be put down because she had entered the island without permission.

The only alternatives were to send her back to France or put her into quarantine in mainland Britain, even though she'd had a rabies jab.

But Anthony appealed to the island's Department of Agriculture and Fisheries, and after an anxious 24 hours they relented and let her stay.

Relieved Anthony added: 'She's doing fine now and is obviously unharmed by her ordeal.'

CAT-AR 'N' BACK (TEN TIMES)

GLOBE-trotting moggie Ozzy clocked up 63,000 miles after getting lost on a Qatar-to-London jet for TEN DAYS.

Owners Jonathan Boyd and Katie Deacon paid £220 to fly their puss back from the Middle East, but he escaped from his plastic basket.

And when British Airways staff opened the hold at Heathrow the cat had gone. It was assumed he had scarpered during a stop in Bahrain and was given up as lost.

But ten days later, a thin and hungry Ozzy was spotted hiding in the hold. By then he had made the 3,150-mile, seven-hour trip to Qatar and back every day.

Ozzy was reunited with Jonathan and Katie, 27, in Richmond, North Yorkshire. The white and orange-flecked moggie is fighting his way back to health in kennels while serving his six months' quarantine.

Jonathan, 26, who worked in Qatar as a teacher, said: 'We had given up hope of ever seeing him again. He must have used up at least two of his nine lives. We are so relieved that he is safe and well.'

A BA spokesman said: 'If he was registered for BA Miles he would have earned enough to travel free to Rio de Janeiro and back, plus a trip or two to Europe.'

MISSION IMPUSSIBLE

KANE the cat was so homesick when his owner moved that he walked 23 MILES to his old house.

The ten-year-old ginger tom crossed trunk roads and even the M1 to return to Lindsay Sharp's former address.

And when he found the new occupants had taped up the cat-flap he simply moved in with a neighbour.

Worried Lindsay spent £1,000 on adverts to trace Kane around her new home in Barnsley, South Yorkshire.

He was only rumbled three months later when a pal visited her ex-neighbour Elizabeth Butterfield in Birstall, near Leeds, and saw him curled up in the garden.

Lindsay, 28, said: 'It's incredible. I can't imagine how he crossed the M1 – he could have been run over hundreds of times. I'll keep him indoors until he's used to living in Barnsley.'

Pal Alison Dawson, 30, added: 'Kane had been with Elizabeth two months – she thought he was a stray. I phoned Lindsay and she was in tears when she arrived.'

Vet Melanie Spencer said: 'Cats have an inner guiding sense.'

CRATE ESCAPE

A SIX-month-old kitten survived a four-week transatlantic journey trapped in a crate on a ship.

The moggie travelled 4,700 miles from Texas to Aberdeen with no food or water.

It's believed she clung to life by licking condensation off the walls of the 40-foot freight container.

Vets in Aberdeen were astonished the cat – whom they've named Olive, after Popeye's girlfriend – survived the ordeal.

Mark Bayliff, who treated her at Arden Veterinary Hospital, said: 'She is the most poorly cat we have seen who has then lived.'

Olive was trapped in the crate from the U.S. to Felixstowe, Suffolk, where the ship docked. She then endured a rail trip to Aberdeen.

Stunned workers at oil services company National Oilwells found her among the cargo.

Doreen Graham, of the SSPCA, said: 'She must have survived on condensation. She's a fighter.'

Poorly Olive now faces six months in quarantine before she can be given a home.

LOST MOGGIE'S 200-MILE TREK

A LOST cat was reunited with its owners after turning up 22 months later, 200 miles away.

Eli, an eight-year-old tom, left Scott Field and Emily Twist heartbroken when he vanished from their home in Hardingham, Norfolk.

But, in an amazing coincidence, he was found by the RSPCA near Scott's mum's home in Gloucester.

Eli was covered in oil and living as a stray on an industrial estate. The RSPCA cleaned him up and put his photo in the local paper, hoping to find him a new home.

Scott's mum Pat Sage recognised the battle-scarred

moggie because he used to be HER pet when she lived in St Florence, West Wales.

Pat, 53, said: 'I knew it was Eli immediately. The giveaway was a mark on his face where he was shot by someone with an air rifle. I took some of my old pictures of Eli to the RSPCA to prove it was him and they agreed there was no doubt at all.'

Scott, 30, and Emily, 21, rushed to collect the cat after Pat called.

Emily said: 'He climbed on our shoulders the moment we saw him. It's great to have him back.'

Part-time fireman Scott added: 'I thought my mum had lost her marbles when she said he'd been found in Gloucester.'

It is not known how or why Eli went so far, although it is thought he may have been attempting to return to his old home in Wales.

Scott believes he hitched a ride in a delivery van. And Emily said: 'He's always liked sitting in cars.'

FUR WHEEL DRIVE

A COMMUTER drove 30 miles to work, then discovered his pet cat hiding under the bonnet.

Stephen Park motored from his home in Ayrshire to Glasgow with nine-year-old moggie Sage nestled beside the engine of his Mazda.

And web designer Stephen only found the trapped animal after he heard her miaows.

Stephen, 36, of Ardrossan, admitted: 'I couldn't believe it. The car was going normally, but when I parked I heard this faint noise coming from under the bonnet. When I opened it there was the cat just sitting there, looking at me. But she seemed none the worse for her trip.'

Dad-of-one Stephen told how the cat, which belongs to wife Michelle, 32, often sleeps in the wheel arches of his car. But Sage had never crept inside the bonnet before she hid away next to the engine on Bonfire Night.

Stephen added: 'I don't know how she got in, but she may have been cold – or just scared by all the fireworks. The car's engine is two-litre and it can get quite hot, but she seemed perfectly fine. Her belly was a bit warm, but otherwise she seemed happy enough.'

Stephen – who has a nine-year-old daughter Jasmine with his missus – said: 'Michelle's delighted Sage survived her ordeal. But it may be some time before she climbs back in there again.'

ARSENAL'S AWAY KITT

BOB the cat became an Arsenal kit-ty after sneaking on to their team coach for a 100-mile away trip to Birmingham.

Bob had crept unseen on to the bus at the Gunners'

Hertfordshire training ground on Saturday, and hid among the kit bags throughout the journey.

He stayed in the hold until the coach stopped at the hotel where Arsenal stayed before their 4–0 Premiership victory over Birmingham City.

When the doors opened, Bob tried to flee, but he was cornered by players in the car park of the New Hall Hotel in Sutton Coldfield, West Midlands.

A disc on his collar gave the phone number of owner Di Clark, 55, who lives near the London Colney training HQ.

Assistant physio Colin Lewin rang Di to say that nine-month-old Bob was safe. Then he let the cat spend the night in the bathroom of his room – after a meal of fish and milk.

An Arsenal official drove Bob home to mum-of-six Di. She said: 'Arsenal have been fantastic. He had been looked after brilliantly by Colin. He said Bob had been very well behaved. But he gets in loads of scrapes.'

BAGH-PUSS

MIRACLE moggie Gracie escaped war-torn Iraq by stowing away in a British Army tank.

The tiny black-and-white kitten took six weeks to complete the sea journey to Britain when the unit's tanks were loaded aboard a ship.

It is believed she survived the ordeal by eating bugs and lapping up moisture from the vehicle's walls.

Troops found Gracie at Southampton docks, from where she was taken to recover at a quarantine cattery.

She is thought to have crept into the tank somewhere near Baghdad. The unit then crossed hundreds of miles of desert to Saudi Arabia before returning to Britain.

Gracie's handler Faith Grant said: 'She was just skin and bone when she arrived. It's amazing that she survived at all, being so young. She was so tiny and we had to feed her milk through a syringe.'

Gracie is called 'the kitten of mass destruction' because she is so lively.

Faith, 21, of the Willowslea Farm cattery at Heathrow Airport, said: 'She's never still and turns the place inside out.'

Once her quarantine spell is over, Gracie will be found a new home.

CAT'S CAR ROOF RIDE AT 60MPH

DAREDEVIL moggie Joe proves you can't keep a cat off a hot tin roof – even after he ended up clinging to it as his owner drove at 60mph.

Staff nurse Adria Bryan was baffled by other drivers flashing their lights at her as she sped along an A-road to work.

Finally, the mum pulled over, and was stunned to find the 14-year-old pet on top of her Ford Escort.

He had been asleep when she set off from home in Rhyl, North Wales, and held on for FOUR MILES.

Adria, 44, said: 'I must have been doing 60. Joe clung on for dear life with his claws to the groove at the top of the rear door. It's unbelievable.'

FUR FROM HOME

A TINY kitten was left fur, fur away after stowing away under a car bonnet – for 133 MILES.

The intrepid moggie climbed on to the engine while the car's owner was on holiday in Campbeltown, Argyll. But she was only discovered when the driver returned to Glasgow and heard miaowing noises from his motor.

The man handed the kitten, now named Chloe, to pet charity PDSA in the city.

Veterinary nurse Therese Gillanders said: 'Chloe was very dirty and scared, but had no real injuries. All she needed was to be looked after properly for a couple of days and given a little TLC. She was a bit dehydrated after the journey, but nothing that some food and water couldn't help cure.'

Chloe was taken in by student nurse Laura Dickson, of Cathcart, Glasgow, and is being looked after by Laura's parents Jim and Anne.

Jim said: 'I've never been much of a cat-lover, but Chloe is like another child to my wife.'

CHAPTER 11

FURR-OCIOUS BEASTS: THE BIG CATS STALKING BRITAIN

THE BEAST OF BRENTWOOD

POLICE have issued an official alert over a panther stalking the Essex countryside.

The big black cat – known as the Beast of Brentwood – was spotted prowling in a field by a PC driving along a country lane.

The beast is known to have killed two geese whose bodies were found at a farm in North Weald. It has also left behind the carcasses of several pigs, and ripped the head from a calf. A farmer's dog was attacked and needed more than 50 stitches.

Expert veterinary pathologist Dr Ranald Munro, 55, scrutinised the dead geese. He said: 'There were large claw marks on them. This is not a dog or a fox, but something much bigger, like a panther.'

Michael Thurgood, who owned the dead geese, said he knew immediately that the birds had not been killed by a fox.

He added: 'Two 12lb birds had been carried over a 4-foot fence and a fox couldn't do that.'

There have been numerous sightings of the beast in

the past few months. Cops advised anyone who sees the panther to remain calm.

A spokesman added: 'Screaming or running away would encourage it to pounce. Left alone it is frightened of humans. Do not approach it.'

Police have called in London Zoo's big cat expert Quentin Rose to help them track down the beast.

TERROR AS JAMES, 13, SEES 'TIGER'

A BOY has reported the second sighting of the 'Doncaster Tiger'.

James Sutcliffe, 13, claimed the creature was in a field close to where a farmhand said a big cat pounced on his truck.

Sobbing James rode a mile on his bike to alert South Yorkshire police.

He said the animal was at least 6 feet long, with a pale yellow striped coat and enormous paws.

PANTHER MAULED ME SAYS JOSH, 11

A BOY of 11 has told of his terror after becoming the first victim of ferocious big cats stalking Britain's countryside.

Josh Hopkins was savaged by one of the panther-like creatures as he played in a field yards from his village home.

The snarling 5-feet-long beast LEAPT at him, sank a CLAW into his cheek, and then clamped the youngster's head in its JAWS.

Screaming Josh managed to free himself and fled home sobbing. Sporting three-inch claw marks on his cheek, he said: 'It was big and black – I thought it would kill me.'

A massive hunt was under way for the creature, which experts fear COULD maul a child to death.

Police warned villagers in Trelleck, near Monmouth, South Wales, to be on their guard. The attack comes after several reports of huge black cats on the loose in the area.

Similar creatures have been sighted across Britain for more than a decade, including the notorious Beast of Bodmin.

Josh was 100 yards from home when the cat – its mouth encrusted with blood from a recent meal – pounced. He said: 'I was on my way home after playing in my den in the woods when I saw a black tail. I thought it was my pet cat Sylvester. I was about to reach down when I realised it was the biggest black cat I've ever seen.'

He went on: 'It turned and made a horrible hissing sound, then reared up and lashed at me with its paw, holding my cheek for a second. The animal had blood on its jaws and I could smell its breath. Then it got my head in its jaws and bit me. I started screaming and ran. The animal ran into fields.'

Mum Rosemary, 42, who has two other children, heard Josh yelling: 'I've been attacked by a big black cat.' She said: 'I thought he meant an ordinary cat until I saw the wounds.'

Josh was treated at a nearby clinic and given antibiotics. Police aim to track down the beast using a helicopter equipped with heat-seeking gear.

Chief Inspector Nigel Russell confirmed: 'It's the first time we've heard of anyone being attacked.'

Big cat expert Danny Nineham, 39, who is helping the hunt, said: 'Josh is extremely lucky to be alive. I'm baffled the creature backed off.'

PUMA HUNTED AT HOSPITAL

A BIG cat hunt has been sparked after four terrified nurses spotted a puma stalking hospital gardens.

The workers described the beast as 5 feet long and 4 feet high. One nurse said she saw the large, tan-coloured cat with pointed ears sitting on a rock in the grounds of Merchiston Psychiatric Hospital in Johnstone, Renfrewshire.

A police spokesman said: 'There were two sightings of it in the wooded area overlooking the hospital, so we don't believe it was a figment of someone's imagination.'

Patients were locked in as a helicopter with heat-seeking devices and a squad of Land Rovers were sent in to track down the feline.

A vet armed with tranquilliser darts was put on standby. The spokesman added: 'Officers did a ground search and a helicopter scanned the area, but search attempts were unsuccessful.'

PANTHER BIT MY CAR

TERRIFIED Gill Bonell called in cops after her car was damaged by what is thought to be a PANTHER.

The vehicle's wing mirrors had huge bite marks, part of the bumper was ripped off, and the mud-flaps were chewed. Paw marks were also left above the Rover's front-left tyre.

Mum-of-three Gill thought vandals were to blame – until police pointed out the paw marks.

She said: 'I'm shocked, stunned, outraged and amazed the same time. Police think it was a panther attack and I'm worried because I have children and our pet cat is missing.'

Gill, of Knowle Gate, Shropshire, added: 'I thought somebody had taken a hammer to the car when I saw the vehicle, the damage was so bad.'

A theory is that the panther savaged the car in a bid to get to the cat hiding underneath.

Wild animal experts have checked copies of the paw prints and scientists are also testing blood taken from the scene.

A police spokesman said: 'We are not wildlife experts, but cannot rule out that a panther caused the damage. The attack carries all the hallmarks of an incident involving a big cat.'

THE BEAST OF, ER, SYDENHAM

COPS are hunting a big cat that mauled a former soldier – in a city suburb.

The 5-feet-long jet-black beast, thought to be a panther, struck in Sydenham, South London.

Tony Holder was attacked after saving his pet moggie from the creature in bushes at the rear of his garden in the early hours.

Dad-of-three Tony, 36, said: 'I could just make out our cat Kitkat under another animal. I kicked out at it, gave it a good boot. A split second later it leapt on me and sent me sprawling on my back in the bushes. I couldn't roll it off me. It was mauling me with its claws and making this terrible hissing and snarling cry. Its huge teeth and the whites of its eyes were inches from my face. I was terrified and fighting for my life. I was grappling with it for a good two minutes before it ran off.'

Builder Tony was left with a five-inch scratch on his face, a bitten finger and a cut wrist.

Armed police searched the area and one officer reported seeing a black labrador-sized animal.

Tony's wife Joy, 32, said: 'He was wonderfully brave.'

Police warned people not to approach the creature. Big Cat watcher Danny Bamping said: 'It sounds like a melanistic leopard, known as a black panther.'

CHAPTER 12

OTHER TAILS: PAMPERED PUSSES AND ASSORTED STORIES

FLASH HAIRY

CRAFTY Elizabeth Broadhurst, 57, gets her deaf cat in every night by flashing her car headlights on and off in Farnham, Surrey.

PURRTY POOPER

PAMPERED cat Cherry Pop was driven in a stretch limo to a £13,000 party on a yacht for her 14th birthday.

The 150-guest bash was laid on by millionaire owner Huey Vanek in Fort Lauderdale, Florida. But the bored Persian red cat just slept.

DEAD TIRED

SCAMP the cat sleeps so soundly by the road at Kingswinford, West Midlands, her owner had to put up a sign saying: 'This cat isn't dead.'

DODGE KITTY

CUNNING Tracey McGhee, 29, has built cat Angel a 20-foot chute from an upstairs window so it can avoid a dog outside her home in Mildenhall, Suffolk.

FIRST AD IS THE CAT'S WHISKAS

BRITAIN'S first TV commercial aimed at cats has been hailed as a purr-fect treat.

The 40-second ad for Whiskas cat food featured shots of fish, mice and birds, with a soundtrack of tweets and squeaks.

Afterwards, scores of pet owners rang *The Sun* to tell how their moggies miaowed and pawed the screen when it came on during *Coronation Street*.

Car washer Jonathan Frost, 26, of Sheffield, said his tabby Spider, aged two, knocked the TV off its stand.

He said: 'He took a flying leap when he saw the little mouse.'

Fara Block, 25, of Ilford, Essex, said: 'My cat Smudge went round the back of the set trying to find the fish.'

Even dogs were dazzled. Lynn Whittenbury, 27, of Long Sutton, Lincolnshire, said: 'My Border collie cross Sweep barked all the way through. Perhaps she thinks she is a cat.'

But there were also some cat critics. Helen Sinclair, 45,

of Harrow, North London, said: 'My five moggies were underwhelmed. They ignored the ad and carried on licking themselves or sleeping.'

CAT AND MOUSALA

HARRY the Persian cat prefers spice to mice, so he lives on a diet of CURRY.

The ten-year-old tom developed his amazing craving after scoffing the remains of a chicken tikka masala left by owner Lea Garrett.

Since then he has turned up his nose at traditional cat food and will eat only Indian nosh.

The barmy moggie's favourite treats include balti chicken, pilau rice, and even red-hot dishes like Madras and vindaloo.

And remarkably, after six months of spicy meals, he is none the worse for wear.

Lea, 27, said: 'Harry's just mad about curry. It's become his staple diet. It started when a half-eaten takeaway vanished from my kitchen. I couldn't work out where it had gone until I saw old Harry sitting in the corner looking mischievous, with curry sauce all over his nose.'

Lea, a photographic technician from Stourbridge, West Midlands, added: 'These days I just have to walk in with a takeaway or cook my own curry and Harry runs up to me purring. Once it's in his bowl it disappears in seconds. He doesn't seem to have any harmful effects, though he drinks lots of water after a vindaloo.'

Bob Partridge, secretary of the British Veterinary Hospital, said: 'Any food that gives cats the proteins they need will appeal to the animal – even chicken curry. However, the spices could cause stomach upsets, so Harry might need other foods to balance his diet too.'

PURR-FECT PAD

SAM the cat is such a stud his owners have built him a luxury love palace in the garden – with a harem of FOUR females to keep him feline frisky.

His pad has a giant bed, carpets, heating, pictures and even a TV on which to watch his favourite soccer.

Kittens fathered by Sam, a Bengal leopard cat, sell for hundreds of pounds. Owner Irene Khajevand, of Slough, Berkshire, said: 'He deserves to live like a king.'

36HR CAT SEARCH TAKES BISCUIT

FIRE crews searched for 36 HOURS for a 'lost cat', then found that the mystery miaowing was coming from a novelty moggie-shaped biscuit tin.

Its owner Janet Gilroy, 67, of Chelmsford, Essex, said: 'I felt awful.'

MY PUSS ONLY EATS PURR FRY

FUSSY cat Schimmy is costing owner Sam Kinsey a packet because he will only eat Chinese meals.

The seven-year-old moggie got a taste for oriental nosh after polishing off a chow mein takeaway bought by student Sam, 18.

Now the picky pussy turns his nose up at canned pet food and sits waiting for helpings of stir-fried noodles, chicken and prawns.

Cash-strapped Sam reckons she will have to get a part-time job to finance the white cat's zany diet.

She said: 'It began when I left the prawn chow mein and went to answer the phone. When I got back Schimmy was purring with delight and licking his paws. All the food had gone. I'm a takeaway fanatic myself and eat Chinese probably five nights a week. But I started making the mistake of leaving Schimmy a little dish of what I had each night. Within days I'd noticed he had stopped eating his tinned food and would only have what I brought home. If I didn't give him some, he would get moody and aggressive. So I started getting him small portions of chicken or prawn chow mein, and now he's addicted. He'll only eat Chinese.'

A-level student Sam, who lives alone in a flat in Walsall, West Midlands, added: 'He will even nibble prawn crackers as a form of dried food.'

Dr Freda Scott-Park, of the British Veterinary Association,

said of Schimmy's choice of food: 'It is strange, but not at all harmful to him.'

PUSSED AS A NEWT

JOEY the cat has developed a drink problem after sneaking off to the pub at night and lapping up a tipple or two.

The moggie got ratted on Bacardi Breezers, lager and cider during his secret binges.

And when worried owner Katie Perfitt, 22, took him to the vet, she was told his liver was swollen from alcohol abuse.

Katie revealed: 'The vet said, "This is going to sound silly but he doesn't drink, does he?" Then he put Joey on antibiotics and told me to keep him on the wagon. From now on the only thing he'll be drinking is milk.'

The one-year-old puss got a taste for booze on nightly trips to The Teal Arms, 50 yards from his home in Ingleby Barwick, Cleveland.

Smitten regulars had taken to slipping him the odd tipple, but nursery nurse Katie had no idea.

She said: 'He was a nutter when he came back – totally hyper, like the cat in the TV ads for Bacardi Breezer. He'd attack the duvet on my bed, then jump on my plate while I was eating. Next minute he'd be flat out snoring his head off and nothing would wake him. I couldn't work out what was wrong.'

Eventually she spotted black-and-white Joey making a beeline for the bar, and followed him.

Katie said: 'The landlady asked, "Is that your cat?" When I asked why, she said, "Well, he's a regular. He's in here every night helping himself to everyone's drinks."'

Now licensee Lynne Thomas, 48, is helping Joey dry out. She said: 'He's such a little cutey, but he's definitely barred.'

Katie added: 'He's fine now, thank goodness.'

PASS THE CAT-CHUP

CHINA the cat has given up her saucers of milk in favour of a daily dollop of TOMATO KETCHUP.

The puss loves lapping up the sauce and winds up with bright red whiskers.

Owner Gemma Downing, 18, got the feline something was up when China tried to snaffle a plate of bacon sarnies smothered in ketchup.

She assumed her pet was after the bacon, but then caught the saucy puss licking blobs of ketchup from the side of a bottle.

Now Gemma has to put out a plate of the savoury substance each night to satisfy the eight-year-old Persian's craving.

Gemma, a student in heritage studies, said: 'I found China up on her hind legs frantically licking up remains of the sauce around the bottle neck. Now she can't get enough of it. Her favourite brand is Heinz and it's really funny to see her licking her lips when I get out the bottle from the cupboard. She starts purring and rubbing herself against my legs.'

Gemma, of Wollaston, West Midlands, added: 'It's costing me a packet to keep her supplied and her white fur gets covered in it. But I love her, so it's worth it.'

Cat expert Dr Freda Scott-Park said: 'I've never heard of this. But cats love strong, smelly food and can soon become addicted to things. The ketchup certainly won't do her any harm.'

CAT TAKES TURN FUR THE WORSE

MOSES the cat must be Britain's most miserable moggie – he's allergic to his own FUR.

His nose was running when owner Claire Dunwell, 24, brought him home from a pet rescue centre.

Moses, aged two, also had weepy eyes before he began sneezing and sniffing constantly.

Vets told Claire her pet had a common cat cold, but a course of antibiotics failed to help. So she took him to animal allergy experts, who diagnosed that the problem was his fur and skin.

Claire, of Wakefield, West Yorkshire, said: 'I loved Moses as soon as I saw him. He had runny eyes, but I was assured there was no infection. Over the next few days I was astounded when he started sneezing all over the house. I had to follow him and clean up after him. When I picked him up, he left silver trails down my clothes. It's like having a baby.'

Writer Claire is now trying out a skin ointment which is applied once a week.

Janice Culligan, of Yorktest Veterinary Services in York, said Moses sneezes because he is breathing in particles from his fur and skin, called dander. When he licks his fur, the dander gets on his tongue, sparking another allergic reaction.

Janice said: 'It's similar to a person with hay fever, but it's all year.'

I'M THE TAP CAT

A WATER-loving kitten has left her owners with a sinking feeling by mastering how to turn on their TAPS.

Cindy and Gerry Falloon keep coming home from work to find the moggie all soggy after taking showers in their three sinks.

Three-month-old Izzy leaves the taps gushing all day long in their kitchen, toilet and bathroom.

Shopworker Cindy, 65, of Alresford, Hampshire, moaned: 'There's never any hot water left for us. Two sinks have lever-style taps, but Izzy even opens the traditional kitchen taps with her paws.'

Filling station attendant Gerry, 68, said: 'We hope it's just a phase Izzy's going through.'

MOGGIE PADDLE

MIAOW'S about that! Custard the cat has amazed his owner by taking up swimming.

The soggy moggie does lengths in a hydrotherapy pool built for DOGS.

Proud Sue Slade takes the tom for 15-minute dips twice a week. She said: 'I know cats are supposed to hate water, but Custard has really taken to it.'

Sue, 55, who runs a property management business, hit on the idea of hydrotherapy for her 18-month-old pet after he kept falling over and a vet diagnosed weak hind legs.

A pal whose dog suffered from a similar condition told Sue how swimming could help. Now Custard loves nothing more than his trips to the pool at St Andrew's Farm Kennels in Brooks Green, West Sussex.

He wears a special harness as he does the moggie paddle, miaowing with pleasure.

Sue, of nearby Warninglid, said: 'Custard's legs are now so strong he can even jump up on to the kitchen table. I'm delighted.'

Kennel boss Annie Silver, 46, said: 'It's the first time a cat has been in our pool.'

Animal expert Dr Roger Mugford said: 'Cats can swim –

but only do so in an emergency if they fall in. In this case, the fact the water is warm is probably a help.'

CATS TURN WOMEN INTO SEX KITTENS

WOMEN cat owners can catch a bug from their pets that turns them into man-eaters.

Scientists say a parasite that lives in cats can infect people and may dramatically alter their personalities.

Women get the 'sex-kitten effect' from the toxoplasma gondii bug, making them fun-loving, desirable, sexy and more unfaithful.

But it leaves men feeling grumpy with the 'alley cat effect'. They become more aggressive, scruffy, anti-social and less attractive to women.

There are about eight million cats in the UK and up to half the human population is said to carry the bug.

The study was carried out at Charles University in Prague by Professor Jaroslav Flegr as part of worldwide research into toxoplasma. He tested 300 people and found that women with the bug were more attractive than those without it.

He said: 'They were more easy-going, warm-hearted, had more friends and cared about how they looked. They were also less trustworthy and had more relationships.' He found that infected men were more likely to brawl and be jealous.

Once the bug is in your body the number of toxoplasma cells grows steadily, meaning women get randier and men get grumpier.

Martin Condliffe, boss of the Ark Pet Centre in West Horsley, Surrey, said: 'This research doesn't surprise me. A number of my cat-owning customers fit the description of sex kitten and alley cat.'

Cat-loving Tory MP Ann Widdecombe cast doubt on the research after hearing the bug could make her desirable and promiscuous.

The 55-year-old said: 'Nobody could apply those adjectives to me.'